Life Laughs

Also by Jenny McCarthy

*Belly Laughs: The Naked Truth About
Pregnancy and Childbirth*

*Baby Laughs: The Naked Truth About
the First Year of Mommyhood*

Life Laughs

The Naked Truth About Motherhood, Marriage, and Moving On

Jenny McCarthy

DUTTON

DUTTON
Published by Penguin Group (USA) Inc.
375 Hudson Street, New York, New York 10014, USA
Penguin Group (Canada), 90 Eglinton Avenue East, Suite 700, Toronto,
Ontario M4P 2Y3, Canada (a division of Pearson Penguin Canada Inc.);
Penguin Books Ltd., 80 Strand, London WC2R 0RL, England;
Penguin Ireland, 25 St. Stephen's Green, Dublin 2, Ireland
(a division of Penguin Books Ltd.);
Penguin Group (Australia), 250 Camberwell Road, Camberwell, Victoria 3124,
Australia (a division of Pearson Australia Group Pty. Ltd.);
Penguin Books India Pvt. Ltd., 11 Community Centre,
Panchsheel Park, New Delhi - 110 017, India;
Penguin Group (NZ), cnr Airborne and Rosedale Roads, Albany, Auckland 1310,
New Zealand (a division of Pearson New Zealand Ltd.);
Penguin Books (South Africa) (Pty.) Ltd., 24 Sturdee Avenue,
Rosebank, Johannesburg 2196, South Africa

Penguin Books Ltd., Registered Offices: 80 Strand, London WC2R 0RL, England

Published by Dutton, a member of Penguin Group (USA) Inc.

First printing, May 2006
10 9 8 7 6 5 4 3 2 1

Copyright © 2006 by Jenny McCarthy

Illustrations by Grant Pominville (www.artbygrant.com)

All rights reserved

 REGISTERED TRADEMARK—MARCA REGISTRADA

LIBRARY OF CONGRESS CATALOGING-IN-PUBLICATION DATA
has been applied for.

ISBN 0-525-94947-X

Printed in the United States of America
Set in ITC Garamond Light with display in Arial Rounded Bold

Evan

The stars are whispering again . . .

Love, Mommy

Contents

Contents

Contents

Contents

Acknowledgments

I would like to give thanks to the women out there who have supported me through the years and who have now become loyal readers. I've done so many things in this business and writing books has brought me the most joy. When you approach me in malls and tell me how much I made you laugh while reading my books I get the chills and smile so much that people think I just got done smoking a big joint. Thank you from the bottom of my heart and I hope I can continue to make you laugh as we both grow old in this world together.

Love, Jenny

Life Laughs

Life . . . Sometimes You Just Gotta . . . Laugh

 ey, welcome back! This book is dedicated to those days when we wake up late for work, feeling fat, gossiped about, screamed at by our children, and not fully adored and nurtured by our horny men. If you are a first-time reader of mine, I need to give you the usual warning when it comes to my point of view on things. I always tell the truth, and that means the whole truth. This book will knock some of you off

your chairs. It's crude, raw, and sometimes dirty but always honest.

I give you a glimpse into my own battle with Life, my marriage and divorce, sex, motherhood, aging, and even PMS. And I hope that you can relate to the funny, gross, bad, and ugly that always comes with life. So please kick off your shoes and tell your man to shut up for a bit and enjoy a few Life Laughs!

PORK . . . It's What's for Dinner . . . NOT!!

Sometimes I wish it was still caveman days when the men hunted for food and we stayed by the fire combing out our legs and armpits waiting for a dead carcass to arrive. Most girls grow up and easily slide into the domestic duties of the home. I never slid in. I kicked and screamed and was eventually thrown in by my hair.

I remember staring at the stove after I became married wondering what the hell I was going to do. The only thing I had ever used it for was to light my cigarettes. Now I was supposed to actually mix things together and create a meal. That was funny.

Walking into grocery stores I would always head for the frozen food section. This is when I was only responsible for myself. I would grab fifteen Lean Cuisines and call it a week's supply. After I got married, the grocery store looked like Harvard University. I couldn't understand anything. I would stand in the produce section not knowing what half the names were for the vegetables in the bins, let alone how to cook them. I continued to push my cart and stopped at the meat counter. Packages of raw meat would stare at me, and I would pick some up looking for how to cook them and there never were any directions. My mom finally gave me a few recipes for stews and such, but half the time I was too tired from work and up with the baby to try to prepare a feast when I didn't even know how to open the package.

Once you start to cook at home, figuring out what to make for dinner that night can be just as hard as figuring out which candidate to vote for. I go crazy every night!! I'll call my mom and ask her what she made or call my sisters to see what they made. Even if cooking is totally your thing, I guarantee that wondering what to make is a daily dilemma in your life. If you have kids who are picky eaters, then God help you. In my house I would feed my son really healthy steamed foods, and when he went to sleep, I would gorge on pizza or cheeseburgers.

One time I tried to make John a really beautiful meal, but it didn't go too well. I saw a big pork thingy at the store. I think it was a pig's shoulder or something, and I decided to take it home and make BBQ pork sandwiches with it. My mom had gotten me a slow cooker for Christmas thinking it would be easy cooking for me. So I decided to let this pig shoulder thingy be my first try. I threw it in there, put a little salt, a little pepper, and even an onion in it. Wow, now that's some fancy cookin'! I put the lid on and saw that the button had two choices: slow and fast. I remember thinking, Why would anyone want to cook something slow? So I put it on fast and went on my way.

A couple of hours later I came to check on it and it looked awesome. Juice dripping, onions browned—I never thought a pig's shoulder would look so attractive as it did in my pot. So I looked at the clock and saw that it had been at least two hours and figured since I had it on FAST it was probably done. Besides, overcooked pork is not a fun chewing experience, so I threw some barbecue sauce on it, ripped off some chunks, and put it in a hamburger bun with a side of potato salad. I walked over to John and showed him my proud creation of a real meal. His eyes bugged out in delight and he happily devoured the sandwich, saying it was the best sandwich he had ever had. I couldn't even take a bite because I was doing some stupid cleanse at the time, so I had to live vicariously through his bites.

After he was done I threw his plate in the dishwasher and smiled in delight at my domestic victory. About an hour later I heard this awful noise coming out of the bathroom. It sounded like an elephant was being eaten by coyotes. These horrid screams and echoes of cries coming out of a porcelain bowl made me quiver. I honestly thought Godzilla had taken over my bathroom. After about fifteen minutes of screams and moans the door finally opened, and standing there was a pale sweaty skeleton of a man. I said, "Oh no, honey, you've got the flu." He replied with a whisper, "It's not the flu, it's your f*cking pig shoulder."

All I could think of was that he was delirious, because my pork sandwich had looked award-winning. Before I could even respond, he turned around and became friends again with the two-foot porcelain bowl.

I ran into the other room and called my mom. I told her of my proud cooking but that John had gotten sick. She began to ask me what I had set the timer on. I told her on fast for two hours. She started screaming in horror, telling me that fast still means at least eight to nine hours for a big pig shoulder and slow would be about twelve to fourteen. I thought that was ridiculous. Who the hell would cook for twelve hours?

Anyway, it turns out John had severe food poisoning because pork needs to be cooked thoroughly. Who knew? They don't teach you that in school! So the next time you get perplexed about what to make for dinner, call some friends and see what they're making. If you're too lazy, go have your husband run out and grab some takeout. If he bitches and moans, just smile and tell him you have a delicious recipe for barbecue pork sandwiches!

The Mr. Potato Head Syndrome

I used to love playing with Mr. Potato Head when I was a little girl. There was just something so cute about him and empowering about having the ability to control what I wanted him to be that day. "Sorry, Mr. Potato Head, I'm not allowing you to have your mustache today. You have to EARN it!" Yes, even at nine years old I wanted to control my man. It wasn't until years later when I married my own Mr. Potato Head that I realized they don't come with all the parts.

When you first meet your potato he can do no wrong. You see past any flaws or sprouts that stick out. You're even able to get him to believe that you're better than all the other Ms. Potatoes he's known in the past. I remember when I took my potato out for the first time to meet all my friends. Everybody loved him. People saw what I saw in him. Together we made mashed potatoes and people ate us up.

As years passed, when we would go out with friends, I noticed that my potato's jokes weren't as funny as they used to be. Sometimes I was kind of embarrassed by them. Everybody else in the crowd still thought he was hilarious, but I kind of rolled my eyes because I was so used to them. This is pretty normal. Just pay attention to other wives' faces when their own husband cracks a joke or does something stupid. I'll bet you they're not laughing or they're doing that fake laugh to cover up how stupid that thing was that their husband just did.

Another change you might experience is how your potato can seem like the most incredible multitasker in the world . . . OUTSIDE the house! If you've ever had the chance to see your man at work, you might stand back and say to yourself, "Wow, this really kind of turns me on. The way he takes control, how everybody listens to him, and how he gets the job done." The reason this might turn you on is because you never get to see this at home.

He turns into Mr. Potato Head the moment he walks in the door. He saves all of his good stuff for everybody else. Men, for some reason, CANNOT multitask at home. Go ahead and try it if you're a newlywed. Start with something simple like asking him to open a jar that's sealed shut while he's on the phone or, better yet, while he's watching the game. The look of confusion that comes over his face is priceless. Almost as if you are speaking in a different language. Doing two things at once was never meant to be a normal trait in men. Except, of course, if it's during sex and he's squeezing a boob while having sex with you. Multitasking in bed doesn't count.

Watching your potato grow old is yet another joyous ritual in marriage. Some potato's skin might become a little more dingy and his "parts" might not be as fun as they used to be. He might also start to stink. Your potato used to have that "new car smell," but he now has the aroma of stinky sock. You might start to say, "What's going on with my potato? It never used to be like this. Now I'm running around trying to find his parts and having to put them on for him." You soon begin to realize Mr. Potato Head couldn't exist without Mrs. Potato Head. They would honestly cease to exist. And to make matters worse, their parts would not only start disappearing but would eventually start wilting and breaking. Your young, energetic, fun potato is now slowly starting

to move toward the sofa and filling his starchy self with beer and refusing to let go of the remote. Your dreamy Mr. Potato Head has slowly reincarnated into Mr. Couch Potato Head! I should really let the toy company know to start adding a couch and a remote control to each set. Then new generations of young girls can practice different ways of telling their Mr. Potato Head to get off his fat ass and unload the dishwasher.

So if you've experienced these joys already in marriage or any relationship, I hope you can take a sigh of relief knowing that you are not alone. And if you're a newlywed, just be aware that even though you might think you married a stud, in all honesty, he's just another SPUD!

The First Poo

Oh, in the beginning . . . when chivalry was at its peak. What a wonderful time it was. I have finally come to grips with knowing I probably will never see chivalry again. Maybe, just maybe, when I'm eighty and have to be wheeled to a car in my wheelchair, my husband might open the car door for me, but that would be it. Okay, he might remove my dentures and brush them for me, but I can't see him doing anything else.

In the beginning, I was really good at playing the "pretending to be polite and perfect" game. After only about two months, though, I was losing speed and began unraveling. My first struggle was trying to hold in my farts after dinner. We've all been there, driving home; you're pretending to giggle at his conversation when the whole time you're clenching your butt cheeks together, praying for green lights so you can run out of the car. Then once you get out of the car you run like hell, screaming, saying you just saw a spider—and you run behind a tree and blow your ass out.

What about the first poo at his place? Remember that? Trying to tuck it away for a different day but you can't, so you go in his bathroom and spray his aftershave like crazy, trying to cover the smell of death. And I'm sure a few of you have experienced the "Oh, SHIT, it won't flush" scenario. I HATE it when that happens. I've been guilty of the scoop-out-and-toss-out-the-window a couple of times in my lifetime.

But my absolute worst one happened when I was only in seventh grade. I went to my new boyfriend's grandma's house because she wasn't home and we needed a place to make out. I had to go number two so bad and made my way to the bathroom. I kept flushing so he wouldn't hear any accidental farts come out during the process. When my mission was completed I flushed the toilet for the last time and watched it circle and circle and circle and then violently shoot out of the toilet with gallons of water and poo poo coming out. Before I could even grab a towel the floor was flooded and it washed into the living room, which of course had to have WHITE f*cking carpet. I couldn't say anything. I just looked at the damage done, including the look of horror on my twelve-year-old boyfriend's face, and ran like hell.

To this day I still have a problem "dropping it like it's hot" at anybody else's house except mine. Even in my own house I still blame smells on my poor maid: "Damn, honey, don't use the kitchen bathroom because Rosa must've had burritos again last night." It worked until the smell seemed to reappear on Rosa's days off. The ultimate test, when you know you both have made it to a certain "comfort" level, is when he's forced to plunge for you. Now, that's love!

I always thought it was funny to hear men bitch that they are grossed out by their women farting or going to the bathroom. I mean, yes, we're ladies, but it's not like God made our back alley plumbing any different from theirs. Most of the time we're eating the same meal, so if their belly is yodeling, chances are ours will too. Hey, at least we don't take two hours to get it out!

All in all, even though it's gross, I still find it all funny. Maybe because it's such an awkward thing, but knowing that everybody poops just makes me laugh. Tom Cruise poops, Brad Pitt poops, even Oprah poops. Ahh, that makes me laugh. So the next time you make a stinky and your husband gets grossed out, tell him to relax, because if Pamela Anderson can still shit and look hot, so can you!

The One-Uppers!

Fighting in marriage is about as common as having sex. Well, some might argue there's more fighting than sex, but you get the idea. If arguing is done in a healthy way and away from the children, I think it can be a very good thing in a relationship. Sure, Dr. Phil might say "talking things out" is more beneficial than fighting, but we are not all married to Dr. Phil. Sometimes we argue because that's what we are used to.

I've noticed a certain type of argument that has happened in my relationships and I'm sure in some of yours, too; I call it the "one-upper." If you don't know what that means, let me give you an example.

"I'm so tired. The baby was teething all day and then the toilet overflowed, so I had to clean it all up."

He replies, "Oh yeah? I couldn't sleep last night and then got up at four A.M. to go to work and had eighty people asking me questions and I could barely drive home because I was so tired."

Or . . .

"I have the worst stomachache. I feel like I might throw up."

He replies, "Oh yeah? I have the worst headache. I feel like my head is going to explode."

Now, why the hell does this happen? The only thing I can think of, because I do it too, is that we want to be acknowledged for our hard work and get sympathy for our pain. But for some reason we all play this one-upper game about who has it harder. My absolute favorite one was when John would announce that he had washed the dishes. Or if I walked in the door on a special occasion he would make me look around at what he had cleaned up. Men seem to need an instant reward for what they SHOULD do and it drives me crazy. John would say, "Did you see I cleaned the dishes?"

I would reply with . . . "Yeah."

Then he would stand there, dumbfounded, waiting for me to leap into his arms, saying, "WHOOPEE! Thanks, BABY!" I don't care if I was married to Brad Pitt. That would NEVER happen. I never got "WHOOPEE, thanks for doing the laundry" from him. Which is the reason why we one-up each other. How do you fix this? I don't know. Remember, this isn't a self-help marriage book. I have no idea what I'm talking about and need help too. But I do know that this is a very common thing in marriage.

In most relationships there is usually one who is the "I want to talk about this RIGHT NOW" person and the other who is the "I don't feel like talking about this right now" person who usually leaves or does the silent treatment. I'm the person who doesn't like to talk about things right away. I need time to digest an argument and process it before I can really let him have it. John, on the other hand, would follow me around the house until he was blue in the face, wanting to get the issue on the table and deal with it. This was a HUGE challenge in our relationship because it would make our fights turn into "why I run away" instead of the topic at hand. So a friend told us to do a very L.A. thing and go see a marriage therapist to give us the tools to get through our arguments. I was so intrigued by this that I dragged John and myself to see her and it was AMAZING. I highly recommend even a one-stop therapy shop in your lifetime. The therapist discovered that I was the one in the relationship who had to have a time-out. I was the runaway and John was the discusser, so the compromise she came up with was that if John and I started arguing I got to say "Time out" and he had to leave me alone for fifteen minutes. I could go in another room and he couldn't bother me about the topic for a whole fifteen minutes. The shitty part for me was that I only got fifteen minutes when I usually like three days. So when my time was up I had to go back into the room, BUT amazingly in that fifteen minutes we had both calmed down considerably and had new clarity about the situation. I was amazed that this shit worked. If this sounds like you, I highly suggest trying it.

So the next time you're in a pickle, scream "Time out!" or give him some time to digest it. I guarantee it will make the makeup sex a lot more fun!

The Goldfinger

Eighth grade. That was really the year I started having fun with boys. I made out with Mike in the back of an alley, and he shoved his tongue so far down my throat that I gagged, ran home, and then scrubbed out my mouth. It didn't matter if it was gross. It was my first kiss. I sat on my porch that day with flushed cheeks, thinking about myself as his bride and hoping the fairy tales in my head would come true.

When I was a little girl the idea of simply being touched on the hand was more powerful than when a boy squeezed my boob. If our pinkies were connected, the butterflies in my tummy would spin out of control. I was content with this. Kissing and holding hands was climactic enough, but little boys are much different. Their emotions have nothing to do with their actions. They will have feelings of wanting to be around a girl, but all that consumes them from an early age is how in the hell they are going to get us in our underwear. First base is kissing, second is squeezing a boob, third base is dry humping, and the home run at this age is the finger. I remember thinking, in some boy's grandma's basement, This is gross. They have no idea what they're doing, and the look on their face is like they just found the biggest pot of gold in history. This is where little girls realize that our "gold" is more valuable than we had thought. It should be treasured. And we shouldn't let too many people tamper with it, because we don't want our "gold" to get dingy. I was careful from that point on about who got to touch my "gold."

As years passed, getting to home base was no longer simply having a "goldfinger." They finally got us to give in and let the gold digger do its thing. Yet the whole goldfingering thing manifested into foreplay and to this

day is widely used as the only foreplay we get sometimes. What men need to realize—and what we need to
tell them—is that goldfingering is foreplay for THEM. After getting used to a penis, why in the hell do we want to
be warmed up with a finger?

It's not eighth grade anymore!! Why men think this is
our preferred form of foreplay, I have no idea. Sometimes
it feels like he's checking a turkey to see if it's done.

Personally, I think it's a lazy man's foreplay. When
they're too tired to actually go check out the mine face-
to-face, they send in the troops to do the work, usually
that soldier called the index finger. I'm sure your man has
sent the same troop member down there many times.
The hard part is when you're working so hard to get
aroused and he starts with that, you don't want to have to
say stop because then that will completely take away any
morsel of sexual energy that was barely there to begin
with. So we tough it out and get through it. If he ever
does it when I'm PMSing, I usually have no problem
telling him to stop it because he has completely dried up
the gold mine. Which totally happens when they're doing
that quick goldfinger mining that seems to be on high
speed where, for some reason, they think the faster the
better. Um, NO!!!

Now I don't want you to think that any fancy finger

work is being looked down upon, because it's not. If they can use the troops while going down to the mine face-to-face, then that's good stuff. Then it feels like a whole army is having a party down there. It's only when it's the one soldier trying to do the work for all of them that it just doesn't work.

So, if you have a hard time explaining this to your man, have him read this chapter so he can get the hint. Otherwise, tell him to send his soldier to HIS OWN DARK COAL MINE. That should do the trick!

Honey, Your Friend's a Bitch!

Remember when you met your potato for the first time and you told all of your friends about him? They were so excited for you. They would ask you if he had any friends for them and bla bla bla. Then weeks would go by and you really wouldn't talk to your friends that much anymore. All you wanted to do was spend every waking moment with your man. He was in every thought of every part of the day. If women could attach themselves to their man with Velcro during this time, they would.

As time passes, you'll notice that your single friends don't mind not hearing from you anymore. You're not on the hunt anymore, and until they can make a nest like yours they're still flying around picking up different-sized sticks to help build that nest. All it takes is one friend in that group to get hitched and panic sets in among all the birds. I'm sure you and your friends all had weddings within a year of one another. And I'm sure you can name at least one friend who settled for less just so she wouldn't be the last Brady married.

Once you become officially married, going out and partying is much different. Now you have to find a couple you both like. It wouldn't be so tough if you were friends with the bride and he was friends with the groom, but it doesn't happen that often. You have to open your circle to allow new people in. Which, I gotta tell ya, I'm so not into. My friends will even talk about how stubborn I am about my circle. I have a waiting list to get in. I just don't feel like getting to know anybody new. I'm old and happy with my handful. I'm sure you can relate in some way. But to be a good wife, you should at least try and get to know some of the women your husband's friends married. One of them might just turn out to be a new best friend.

I don't know why this is, but there is always one girlfriend of yours that your husband hates. I don't get it. He says she's either a slut or a bitch, and when you tell him you're going out with her, he rolls his eyes or makes some kind of comment. This is really funny. Why do they care so much? And if "that" friend is part of girls' night out, watch your husband get crabby and make you call him during the night. It's almost as if he doesn't trust you around this girl and he worries that bad wife behavior might slip off this girl's skin and accidentally enter your body. What does he think is going to happen? A runaway dick is going to be flying through the air and your friend is going to catch it and shove it up your vagina? Guys need to understand that when we go out with our friends we don't give a shit about guys. We just want to drink, make fun of what others girls are wearing, and bitch about our marriages. We're not looking to see if we've still "got it." We know we've "got it." We're just having a good time with the pussy posse.

When guys go out with their friends they seem to lose brain cells and all concept of reality. Unlike girls, men still try to go out to a club to see if they've still "got it." Not to cheat (hopefully), just to see if their feathers are still as alluring to the opposite sex. They'll even talk to some other birds just to show off to their friends that they've still got it. It's so stupid, but I guess it's in their genes to try and attract women until the day they die.

You can't really get jealous of them doing it. It's gonna happen whether you like it or not. Know that penises in numbers equal stupidity and that even if a vagina came flying through the air they would all just stare at it because their brains don't work fast enough to figure out what to do with it.

If We BOTH Bring Home the Bacon, We Should BOTH Fry It Up in a Pan!!!!

If I had been born centuries earlier, I would have been burned at the stake. I don't consider myself to be a hard-core feminist. I just believe in equally pulling the weight. For instance, if I were a stay-at-home mom, I would keep the house running and in order, cook, and bring up my babies, and I would expect my man to work his ass off providing for the family. If I were to work nine to five along with my husband, I think we should both be responsible for the duties at home. He should not be allowed to kick off his shoes and let his stinky feet smell up the room while I run around frying up the bacon we BOTH paid for. Even though I say this, it didn't happen in my home as often as I'd hoped. But you can be damn sure I'll try and make it a reality next time.

The problem I run into when trying to implement this is that men can't do as good a job as we can of taking care of the house. In fact, they just plain suck at it. I know a few husbands who do the cooking, but let's get real . . . not enough. I'm not sure if men purposely suck at home responsibilities or if they're just genetically incapable of doing them. It has to be something in their genetic makeup, because when we both would come home from work, I would run to the baby and hug him and take care of his needs. The other half would go check his e-mails and then come see the baby. I think the male species is still stuck in the caveman days. They know how to go out and hunt for food, come home, have sex, take a dump, pat their kid on the head, and go to bed. It's just not fair. Then they actually are upset that we don't want to have sex after the baby goes to sleep. Sometimes I used to purposely not shower just to keep him away. I am physically too exhausted by the end of a hard work day to try and fake orgasms.

The only way I was able to finally show John how much extra work I was doing was to completely stop doing all the extra work. I stopped cooking, I stopped doing the dishes, and I stopped doing the laundry. He couldn't understand what was going on. He thought I was going through some sort of depression. I realized that he couldn't possibly have known how much I was doing simply because I was always doing it. It worked! Well, sort of. When he ran out of jeans to wear he actually went to the store and bought five more pair. I was so pissed, but he definitely got the hint. He started washing the baby and taking the clothes to the laundry room (note how I say taking the clothes to the laundry room, not actually washing them). This is also where "Bribing for Blow Jobs" can really help you out.

Remember that television series where the wives swapped with other wives and the husbands always wound up crying because they had to do all the chores their wives usually did? It's kind of the same theory. You can't just bitch to them about all the things you do; you have to take it away for a bit so they can appreciate your efforts.

So if you've got an old-fashioned husband who still expects you to do everything and work all day, I feel sorry for you. At least make sure there is one night of the week or at least part of a weekend that is YOUR time. If you lose your sense of self and become a slave to household chores you might become a pretty sad wifey, and you can't be a good wifey or a good mother if you are not taking care of you!

Bribing for Blow Jobs

All right, let's talk about the one thing men love to talk about: their penis, their rod, their purple sword, their giant shaft, and their absolute favorite word for it . . . their "cock." That name bothers me, for some reason. My ex-boyfriend would constantly talk about his cock. Personally, I thought it deserved more of a name like "pinky toe" than cock. Oh, come on, you've all been with at least one guy where you felt nothing while he was ramming you, like he was digging for oil with his pencil dick. Then he would try to do that circle technique where his hips would circle around and around just to get all sides to touch. GROSS!!!

I've always wondered if I am the only person who thinks penises are somewhat unattractive. Don't get me wrong, the right one can feel awesome, but the overall look of them is, well . . . just funny.

The first time I saw one was when I was thirteen. A boy pushed my hand down there, and I remember thinking EW! It was throbbing and hard and seemed like a monster on a mission. I didn't know what to do, so I started twirling his pubic hair around with my fingertips.

He said, "What the f*ck are you doing?"

I replied, "Giving you a hand job?"

He pushed my hand away and then broke up with me.

Years later, after somewhat getting the hand job down to a very amateur technique, I was forced to move on to the blow job. And of course the first time I heard about it, I thought, Do you really blow on it? My one slutty girlfriend in school laughed and said, "No, you just put your mouth on it."

Boy, I wish it were that easy!

Maybe you too have heard about those women who say that they LOVE giving blow jobs. Well, I can tell you this . . . those girls either are single or they're porn stars.

Once you're married, LOVING to give blow jobs becomes HAVING to give blow jobs. Can it still be fun? Yeah, of course, but a lot of the time it can feel like a chore. Just like vacuuming!

When John and I were in the "honeymoon years" of our relationship we used to always make sure we warmed each other up for the big game, if you know what I mean. I'll take care of your "bat" if you take care of my "dugout." The sad thing is that most dugouts become neglected as a pregame necessity later on in marriage. Yet us women are STILL giving out blow jobs before the big game without getting any warm-up in return. Why??? Do men think sex is pleasure enough on its own? I personally think NOT. So I finally got smart and decided to stop giving blow jobs until I got something in return. And I don't mean sexual stimulation—I'm talking about getting shit done around the house and rewarding with a blow job or simply . . . "Bribing for Blow Jobs." If you're sneaky about it, your house could be painted by him and the laundry completely done without him even knowing what's up. You have to start off with simple tasks, like asking him to hang a picture. Then tell him how much it turns you on to watch him hammer that nail into the wall, and then slowly unzip his pants and start vacuuming!!

Now I know some of you are probably saying, "I would rather hang the picture myself than have to give a blow

job every time he does something." This is the thing . . .
you stop doing them after each task and only give the reward blow jobs before sex. You carry that task reward into
the bedroom and remind him of it. You still have to give
them anyway, but now he thinks that if he just helps out
around the house a little more his wife will probably give
him a little somethin'-somethin' in return. And the great
thing about giving a blow job before sex is that you don't
have to get him to climax. All you're doing is warming him
up for batting practice and then letting him loose. You
don't have to work so "hard" for his reward.

Mind you, I wish it didn't have to be this way, but let's
"get real." Blow jobs can become a chore, so why not
make your husband share in the "chores"? If I'm working
my ass off to keep the house in order, he'd either better
pitch in or find a pinch hitter, because this dugout is
closed!

Happy Anniversary!

The day I walked down the aisle was truly one of the best moments of my life. If you and I are like most little girls, we begin planning the details at age eight. We've decided on a color palette and even which friends have made the bridesmaid cut before we've even grown boobs.

My wedding was spectacular, but looking back at my own pictures I could still breathe fire remembering all the shit that went wrong that day. Because ALL weddings have something that just doesn't go right. If you're lucky, it's Uncle Bob who can't hold his liquor. If you're not lucky, it's hearing the kitchen staff drop all the trays of food as they are about to bring them out.

I actually got food poisoning the night before my wedding. I ordered a cheeseburger in my hotel room before I went to bed. I had been dieting for so long and I figured the cheeseburger wasn't going to show up on my thighs overnight, so I thought I would treat myself. I became so sick that my fiancé and my mom had to come to the room and spend the night with me. It was kind of funny, though, because there was only one bed, and my mother, my future husband, and I squeezed into it together that night. I wish I had a picture of that experience, but the visual of it in my head should last a lifetime.

For most couples, overspending on your wedding is to be expected. I went f*cking crazy overboard on mine. I maxed out cards, took out a loan, and even made a deal with a European magazine to have exclusive pictures. That totally bit me in the ass because the contract said that if any pics got out they wouldn't have to pay me. So I hired security guards for my wedding to look out for anyone with a camera. I wouldn't allow one guest to bring a camera along because this magazine was paying for almost half the wedding.

The next day we found out that a waiter took secret pictures of the wedding. I was devastated. Let me be honest here for a second. I know I'm not a grade-A celeb, so the fact that this happened to little ole me would be flattering on any other day EXCEPT this one. I got the phone call on my honeymoon stating that the magazine would not pay the tab of my wedding and that it was ALL MINE. I hung up the phone, threw up, and sold my house to pay off the wedding. If you saw me do any really cheesy movies during the year of 1999, just know I was paying off my flower bill.

I was really surprised to see how many bad gifts people give as wedding presents. First of all, I'm from Chicago, and our tradition there is to give cards with money—just like the mobsters in the movies at their wedding. The maid of honor holds a money bag at the end of the greeting line and collects all the cards. I LOVE this tradition. If anyone walked in with a gift you would still, to this day, get a dirty look and then be talked about in the family for a very long time.

When I married John, who was a native Californian, I had no idea that the tradition on the West Coast was to bring gifts. I was expecting some good cash and all we got from his side of the family were ceramic cats and angels that said *God Bless Your Home*. I would love for the rest of the country to go back to the money days. Young couples don't need crystal, they need CASH!! Let's bring it back, people.

I also think anniversary gifts are stupid. Don't get me wrong, any gift can be great, but the anniversary themes like paper and wood are just plain stupid. If you're gonna send anything, send CASH. Write on the card, *Don't worry about your electric bill this month. Happy anniversary.*

Still, my best recommendation is to cuddle up on the couch with Taco Bell and look at your wedding photos. I'm telling ya, if you haven't tried it, sitting around talking about Aunt Fro's wig can be more fun than anything.

Until Death Do Us Part

I was only thirteen when I met Tony, my high school sweetheart. We saw each other for the first time on the city bus coming home from school, and he took my breath away. I remember telling my mom that I loved him, and like all moms do when their daughter is only thirteen, she said, "You're not in love, you just have a crush. And by the way, you're not allowed to date him until you're sixteen."

I was devastated. He was my soul mate, and our love couldn't wait three more years. So I did what any thirteen-year-old would do in this situation: I lied to my mother for the next three years. Every weekend, "Sarah" and I went to the movies, but in all honesty I was in the backseat of a Toyota, making out and dry humping with my first true love. It was the best time in my life. We dated for almost six years and eventually knew we needed to break up to see what life had to offer besides each other. We met at a White Castle, kissed each other good-bye, and never saw each other again. To this day I'm grateful I got to experience true love when it was in its purest form . . . in my youth. When damage hadn't been done yet and you're not fighting over the gas bill.

Yet how can a simple word like *love* be so powerful in its meaning and cause such happiness and pain? It requires so much work to keep yourself from getting hurt that you either harden up to make the tough times easier or sadly give all of your mojo away, leaving nothing for yourself. Or you might be one of the lucky ones who manage to keep love the first priority in a relationship.

I asked a couple who has been married for fifty years how they have managed to stay together so long. They smiled and looked at each other and then started beating each other with their canes. I'm just kidding. I thought that was a funny visual. Anyway, it was pretty profound.

The woman said that marriage has so many levels to it. And on each level their marriage would always come to a crossroad. That crossroad was either a major fight or simply being bored of each other. And amazingly, when they were forced to face their own shit (my word, not hers), they knew they either had to work on it or run like hell. This couple didn't run. They faced each other, battled it out, and won. They got to go to the next level. They said that being able to overcome something together was very empowering.

So even though there are times you want to run like hell or when you feel stale and bored, remember that opening your heart and refilling it with love just might keep you married long enough to beat each other with canes.

Thou Shalt Not Covet Thy Neighbor's Lawn

Why do we always want what we can't have? I think it's human nature to think that the grass is greener on the other side—especially when it comes to our own bodies or even our jobs. We want what other people have because it simply looks more appealing from our side of the street.

Living in a community where all the houses look alike can make you more envious than if every house is different because the only thing you can change is your landscaping. My mom lives in one of these communities, and it's hilarious to witness every time I go home to visit. Each home has baskets of flowers with bird feeders and fake geese or deer on the lawn. It looks like it rained plastic animals all over the neighborhood. The funny thing is that as soon as someone gets something new and unique for their landscaping, everyone quickly follows, no longer making it special. My mom will pull back her curtain and gasp, "Oh, for Pete's sake, the Kolochowskis bought the gosh-darn life-size flamingo mosquito eater I just put out last week!"

My mom even has a goose on her front step that has a wardrobe for every season. I'm still trying to find a dominatrix outfit for its Halloween costume. A leather crotchless bustier might look pretty good on a plastic goose in a very Catholic Chicago suburb.

Besides drooling over your neighbor's lawn you might find yourself drooling over other wives' "gifts." I can't tell you how many times we've gone out and the wife sitting next to me flaunts her new diamonds at me. Personally, I think BIG diamonds are "sorry I cheated on you" rocks, but the fact that she got a gift and all I got was "Look, babe, I put the toilet seat down for you" makes me feel jealous. It's not that I want diamonds—I just want a little somethin'-somethin' for my blood and sweat too. Shit, I would be happy with a bagless vacuum as a gift.

Being somewhat jealous and envious did make me work harder to keep up with the Joneses. There's always at least one Joneses family on every block. They're the ones with the perfect basketball net and the best pool, the dad has the best in-home entertainment system, and the wife has no cellulite. All of this could make any neighbor drool with envy and run back to their spouse, saying, "Can we get that too?!"

I think, in general, girls might covet more then guys, especially when we are looking in gossip mags. I love living vicariously through J-Lo's new couture outfits or watching the Oscars and picking which dress I would wear and then running to the mall and trying to find the closest knockoff.

We all covet. I personally think it's healthy, especially if it's done to push you forward and make you get shit done, even if it is cementing the seven-foot Jesus statue on your lawn. So when your neighbors start planting their own Jesus statues cuz yours looked so good, simply smile and tell yourself that imitation is the highest form of flattery. Yeah, right . . . don't tell that to my mom.

No, Couches Don't Belong in the Kitchen!

Because I don't know you personally, I have no idea what your taste in house decor is like. But what we can all relate to is how our men think that they are interior designers when it comes to decorating our houses. This is another time in the relationship when if a man just listened and did everything his wife said, they would get along a lot better.

"No, honey, the stuffed dead owl does NOT look good on top of the toaster oven!!"

"No, people do NOT want to walk in and see an iguana tank next to the front door."

"NO, I don't care if your grandma's ashes are inside the ceramic toucan bird painted all colors of the rainbow. It's NOT going next to our bed!"

I give men real credit for trying, but if you hold some sort of power, this is where you can and should usually win. If you're married, think back to when you registered for your wedding gifts. You both walked around with that laser gun, and he clicked on items that looked like garage-sale giveaways or things that you had absolutely no need for. "John, we do NOT need dishes in the shapes of different countries." He replies with "But you said you wanted some china," and he holds up a plate in the shape of China.

Hopefully, by this time, you've both come to an agreement with at least a theme. Whether it's Mediterranean or country or my personal favorite: whatever-the-hell-was-the-cheapest-thing-we-could-find theme or my other favorite: it's all my college stuff. It's up to us girls to make our home LOOK like a home. If the guys want to hang up their fluorescent beer-light fixtures, do it in the basement. Give them at least one room to f*ck up. If you don't have a basement, give him the garage. Garages are a great place for your husband. It's not a place your girlfriends are ever interested in checking out, so have him hang his dead animal up in there.

Furniture placement was another sticky area in our household. John really wanted to be part of the placement. His ideas were just bizarre. Sometimes you can look at a room and simply see where everything should go. Long wall usually means sofa wall and short wall means TV wall. Oh, no, not in this house. The short wall didn't have enough room to hold our couch, yet John insisted that it made it look cooler even though it took up twice the room. And the rug shouldn't go in the middle of the room—it should go against the wall. Then we fought about lighting. He wanted to put colored lightbulbs in. Can you believe it? Someone could have come over and said, "Jenny, why are you feeling so blue today?"

"I'm not blue, silly, it's our F*CKING BLUE LIGHT-BULBS!"

It finally got to the point where I started flashing him so I could have the couch in a certain spot. You should have seen what I had to do to put the TV where I wanted.

So if you're in a pickle when it comes to your man and house decor decisions, you can either battle it out or show a little nipple. Personally, it's a lot easier to get naked.

You Don't Bring Me Flowers . . . Anymore

D o you ever go to the bookstore and see the romance novels—you know, the ones that used to
have Fabio on the cover? I used to think, Who the hell
buys these? I asked my publisher and she said A LOT of
women. Why do you think there are so many of them?
So for a second there I thought maybe I should write one
of those next. If women are in such need of romance,

maybe I can contribute something in that part of the writing world. Here is a sneak peek at what I would write. . . .

Michael bursts through the door looking sexy as f*ck.

"Samantha!"

He walked toward me and threw me to the ground.

"Ow, my head."

"Sorry," he replied.

I didn't care that my head was bleeding. My heart ached to be touched by this soul.

He climbed on top of me and started kissing me passionately. I felt my labia start to swell. I couldn't take the amount of heat radiating between our two souls any longer. I slid my nails into the strong, lean part of his back. He began to scream, "AHHHHH!!"

One of my fake nails was lodged into his back. I turned to him and slowly removed it with my teeth. I could tell that this made Michael's heat get very erect. He slowly rose above me to show me his hard manhood. I stared in awe and slowly began to move my mouth closer to it. Just as my tongue was about to touch it, I suddenly stopped and said, "What is that?"

He looked down at his manhood and saw a large blister on it.

He smiled reassuringly and said, "It's a love blister, darling."

I looked at him and smiled. "Just like mine." And pointed to the one on my lip.

"Oh, Michael, I always knew we were meant for each other."

Do you think there's a market for comedic Harlequin novels? Probably not. Anyway, once you get past the honeymoon phase of a relationship, romance seems to get phased out. Ask most of your married friends if they even make out during sex anymore, and most of them will say, "No, we don't." Even though most women crave it and want to make out, we have to feel in a romantic mood. But after being in a relationship for so long, sometimes sex becomes a way to get off instead of lovemaking. Romance is different and you actually have to work at it. Romance requires imagination and creativity. Unfortunately, most married sex lacks this completely—unless the guy thinks squeezing your nipples is romantic. If he does, I would start plucking out each one of his pubic hairs, asking him how romantic *that* feels.

The thing about making out is that there are no sexual stimulations in your mouth, so true passion requires feeling in your heart and head. Only then will the butterflies in your belly dance. But if your head isn't in the right place, those butterflies are going on a coffee break. Remember, romance is a two-way street. In order to get some, you also have to give some. So give it a try, and if he doesn't respond, simply start plucking out his pubic hairs one by one. Ouch!

Honey, Where's the Visa Bill?

People say that money doesn't buy happiness—well, they can all kiss my ass. I grew up with hardly any money, and I still seem to be living from paycheck to paycheck. I guarantee that money is the source of many marital fights.

I remember when I was a little girl and the only thing I worried about was what my mom was going to make for dinner. Not the gas bill or even tuition. Even though we didn't have a lot of money, my parents did a good job of hiding their concerns. I'm sure after they put us to bed at night they bit off their nails trying to get the mortgage paid that month. I so miss those days when bills were not my problem. Even when you move out as a young adult you freak out not being able to pay a credit card bill, but it's a different degree of stress. It's a whole lot different when you're married and your baby needs diapers and your credit card is maxed out. Financial stability in marriage is something couples dream of and hope to achieve before they die. It seems that every time we try to build a nest egg something happens, like the car breaks down, and the nest egg is empty again. Why are we always struggling to stay above water? I don't care what anybody says, money has to at least buy a sense of peace.

I was the one in the marriage who was always freaked out about our finances. John is a director, and in the business we are in, we are constantly unemployed. Yes, I make a decent income, but sometimes I can go for months without working and that nest egg disappears quickly. I hated it. We were constantly up, down, up, down. After I had my son I made a promise to myself that anytime someone offered me anything, I would take it. I've got a family. I could care less if people make fun of me because I just did a herpes ointment commercial. (Okay, I probably wouldn't do a herpes ointment commercial, but you get the idea.) (Okay, yeah, actually I would.)

Another financial pain in the ass is wanting to buy things but having to hide them from your spouse. Usually one of you is the spender and the other is the penny-pincher. If you are the spender and still young in your marriage, I highly suggest being the one in charge of writing out the checks every month. This is really the only way to get away with buying things and not having to provide an explanation.

Personally, I think women make better money choices than men. Most men would use their extra money to buy surround sound stereo equipment, while women would at least buy a new dishwasher. Yet he would argue the stereo was more useful for the house.

The one thing I can say about money is that for some reason it always works out. You think you could be at the end of your rope, that there is no way you are ever going to get past this financial woe, and you always wind up pulling through. Sometimes it might require taking a loan from somewhere. But *hopefully* some higher power will make sure you can get to the next month.

So the next time that Visa bill comes in, don't freak

out. Either hide it from your husband or find ways to minimize your shopping sprees. And don't be too surprised if you turn on your television and see me selling some new cream, saying, "Do you need some relief from your genital warts?"

Because I guarantee it's going to happen!

I'm Fat and Saggy and I Have a Huge Zit on My Butt!

Yes, even I am painfully insecure. Don't be fooled by any pictures you might see of me. The airbrushing technology today takes away every freckle, stretch mark, zit, and wrinkle. Not to mention that the computer can actually give a girl completely different boobs. I swear in my last layout I said to the photographer, "Those aren't my boobs." He replied with, "I know, don't they look great? I even lengthened your legs and shaved your thighs." He put somebody else's boobs on my body! Everybody out here is a phony piece of shit. NOBODY in Hollywood looks like they do in pictures. This is why I would love to start adding a disclaimer after every layout. . . .

"Please enjoy, boys, but to just let you know, the stretch marks, the cellulite, and the zit on my ass have been removed for your viewing pleasure."

It's really not fair that perfection is made through computer enhancing. It makes it physically impossible to keep up. I've seen the hottest of the hot out here—Jessica Simpson, Pamela Anderson, Carmen Electra—and they are all pretty girls, but when I look at them I say, "Wow, that's not in the pictures." And believe it or not, these are some of the most insecure girls I have ever met.

I still consider myself to be a Midwestern girl who is living in this foreign world called Hollywood. I'm glad I haven't forgotten my roots and where I came from. I would love to get out and move back and eat ribs and mashed potatoes and hang out at the local bar and play darts, but I have a baby now and you can be sure I'm gonna use this town as much as it's using me. It's still hard, though, because when you break down all of my goofiness and crudeness I'm as insecure as the rest of them. I think my biggest physical insecurity is my stretch marks. If you read my other books you know that I got

hammered by them, and I hate that they just won't go away. They even look like they glow in the dark during sex. The thing that I keep trying to remind myself of is that men love a confident woman. Mind you, I am sure of myself in every other part of my life, but not here. The more confident you are, the more your man will be turned on. But how can I be confident about my stretch marks? Should I shout out in the heat of passion, "Touch my stretch marks, baby, oh yeah, run your fingers over those wavy purple indentations on my thighs!" Um . . . I think it would make him puke.

All right, enough of this woe-is-me shit. Let's talk about getting proactive. I am not a fan of exercise, but it still remains the best way to get your fat, saggy ass in gear. Personally, I took up Weight Watchers. I still get to eat like a girl from the Midwest, but it taught me portion control. Now I feel and look better. I have more confidence.

So just remember, ladies, a confident women is usually a desired woman. Even though you have a white-head zit on your butt and your husband suddenly moves you into the doggy-style position, don't panic! Stay confident and remind yourself that Jessica Simpson gets a few zits on her ass too!

The One Who Holds the
TV Remote
Is the One Who Is in Control!

Since the beginning, men have led the way. They were responsible for the shelter and protection of their families. I'm sure Adam was a real leader, moving branches out of the way for Eve. But even Adam did as Eve told him. She says, "Adam, eat the apple."

He says, "I don't think that's such a good idea.

She says, "Just eat the stupid apple, it's no big deal."

He says, "But there's a snake staring at us. I don't know."

She says, "WILL YOU JUST EAT THE FREAKING AP-PLE ALREADY!!!!"

And so he does.

So even though men might appear to have everything under control, it truly is the women who rule the roost—even if we might make a bad decision once in a while. We are so lucky to live in a time and a place where we are able to speak up without being tortured.

I truly believe having a balance of power is the healthiest kind of relationship. I've met wives who abuse this, though, and their poor husbands are walking around with their tail between their legs. That's not fair, either. Hopefully you are with someone who will let you speak your mind but will not let you walk all over him.

I tend to control too much. I have a problem thinking that if it's not done my way it's probably going to be done wrong, so I wind up doing everything! I really need to learn how to relax and say, "Oh, f*ck it." But I'm years away from doing so.

Now as we all know, there have been some seriously controlling assholes in our history books. Caesar, Napoléon, and the H one. I can't even say his name. Anyway, I honestly believe some women are still married to the reincarnated version. My friend just got out of a pretty controlling relationship. This is an example of where control gets out of control. If your partner is checking your voice-mail mes-

sages, reading your e-mail, telling you what and what not to wear, not letting you go to the gym to work out, and insulting you constantly so he ultimately feels in control, please get the HELL out of the relationship. When I asked my friend why she stayed with him for so long, she said that the more he controlled her and put her down, the more she would try and prove to him that she was good enough for his standards. She also said that she was hoping for change. That's where you can get in big trouble! Most of us already know you can't really change people; they have to want to change. There are millions of women out there stuck in these types of marriages. As you all know, this is not a self-help book, but for the love of God, if this is you, get some help. It took years for my friend to get rid of her Napoléon, and I hope and pray most women have the strength to tell theirs to f*ck off.

Most cases aren't that severe, thank God. I think the majority of power struggles revolve around who gets to hold the TV remote at night. Men usually have it in their hand or near them like it's an extension of their penis, and unfortunately if you feel like cuddling with him while watching a chick flick, good luck. We are usually the ones who have to go to the other TV so we can watch our cheesy reality shows.

Even though we can make men do what we want, it's

important to let your man feel like he's in charge some of the time. So the next time he's hogging the remote and acting like he's in control, just smile and remind yourself that you both wear the pants in the family. His are just stinkier!

I'm Not PMS-ing . . .
You Asshole!!

The worst thing your man can say to you while you're PMS-ing is "You must be PMS-ing!" It can pretty much guarantee something thrown at his face or sex being withheld for an extra couple of weeks. The thing that sucks for me is that I PMS for ten to twelve days before my period. That's almost half a month of me crying or talking to my man with my teeth clenched. And I don't know about you, but it seems to be getting worse the older I get.

I try to remind myself that, as hard as PMS can be, it is also a very spiritual time of the month. You might say things that you never would at any other time, and by getting it all off your chest you accomplish so much that you put off month after month. The Native Americans call it a woman's "moon time." They say we have many spirit guides around us who help us take charge and use this energy to our advantage. Others might call you a bitch during this time, but if you pay close attention, you really do accomplish a lot.

Let's talk about cravings. If you've been a follower of mine and read my last couple of books, you know that I have a HUGE appetite. For those of you who don't know, I gained almost eighty pounds during my first pregnancy, and I still love to throw down a burger. My appetite during PMS feels like I'm on the third week of *Survivor*. I f*cking love food! God, this is making me hungry. This brings me to the topic of eating one of the naughtiest vices during this time of the month, and I don't mean Brad Pitt. I'm talking about chocolate!! I've heard so many theories about why most women crave it, whether it's a sugar pick-me-up or hormonal. I don't really care; I'd lick it off a homeless man's shopping cart if that was the only piece left on the earth.

If you are not a chocolate craver, you're a salt craver during PMS. It's funny when I ask women which they prefer. They respond like it's their team they're rooting for. They might even look at you funny if you're not on their team. Whatever team you're on, I have some very interesting "Jenny facts" about eating during PMS. (By the way, "Jenny facts" are facts found by me on Google or something I heard from friends. Don't ever assume I know what I'm talking about . . . ever!)

So one PMS afternoon I was tearing through my pantry desperately trying to find anything to swallow. I was losing my mind. I started tearing stuff open and gorging. If you have ever seen an afterschool special where they show bulimics gorging food behind grocery stores, that's me . . . every month . . . without the throwing-up part. Sometimes I choke because I forget to swallow, and a couple of times I almost bit off my finger. I'm not kidding. If you ever meet me in person ask me to show you some teeth marks on my finger. Anyway, as I was gorging away, I was pondering why women get SO hungry during PMS. I decided to sit down at my computer and Google it. I typed in *Hungry during PMS*. And to my surprise there was a lot of info on the Web. I found some of the best PMS news ever!!! It said that during PMS women get so hungry because they are burning 500 more calories a day. Our metabolism speeds up, and our body demands more fuel (or potato chips) to get through the day. RIGHT ON!!! That means we can get away with increasing our calorie

intake without gaining the weight. It also means that if you still "watched what you ate" during this time you could possibly lose weight after your period. Do you ever notice sometimes that you actually feel and look a little leaner after your period (besides losing all the water weight)? That's what happens when you don't gorge. But I say screw that. I'm gonna pig out guilt-free.

Besides food, so many other things could throw you off during PMS: a bad hair day, the bitch in the office that looks at you weird, and the biggest one of all . . . your man!!!!!!! I swear to God I can hear the guy cutting his toenails three rooms away. Even chewing with his mouth open or saying stupid stuff like "Did you remember to buy water?" can honestly make me want to tear off his skin and run him over in my car.

So if you've also become a chocolate-craving psycho bitch, just know that it really is okay. And if your man is underneath a car and you're sitting behind the wheel, just smile at the police officer and ask him if he's got any chocolate.

Um . . . Because . . . Um . . . My Vagina Is Sleepy?

Sometimes you're just not in the mood. No, let me take that back. Usually women are too tired to be in the mood. Nowadays it amazes me how much we women have to do to keep our families running smoothly. Unfortunately, saying you're too tired night after night gets old and can cause your partner to think it's him. That's why you need to come up with some better excuses.

The old headache scenario has been done to death, but

if that's all you can think of at the last minute, go with it. But try to be a little more convincing. Don't say you have a horrible headache and then go put on a Walkman and listen to Metallica. You've got to work it a little. Pretend to take some Advil and talk with crunched-up eyebrows. Even request a lay-down while he watches the baby. Being a good actress is necessary when you're using an excuse to get out of sex.

The same acting is required for the bellyache routine. You can't say you are too nauseous for sex and then go make yourself some chili. Go stick a Tums in your mouth and occasionally moan. Even push out a couple of farts and say, "See, I told you."

The only easy non-acting one is to simply go to sleep. Most of the time your husband won't wake you up. He might try a little by poking your leg with his hard-on, but for the most part, if you snooze you don't lose!

I think the only thing women enjoy about getting their period is that it's a solid excuse. The great thing is that it's not even an excuse! They can't blame us at all for "Aunt Flo" coming on what was supposed to be sex night. Occasionally I would hear, "I don't care if you have your period." And I would quickly reply, "GROSS!" It amazes me that men are still willing to go there even though you're flowing like the Nile.

The absolute best excuse, hands-down winner, no way, no how he would want sex from you is . . . the yeast infection. (Read more on these in "Is That a Lobster in Your Pants or Are You Just Happy to See Me?") The only problem with this one is that if you use it too many times he's going to think you have a serious problem with your vagina and will start to stay away from it more than you'd like him to. This is the one I use in desperate need because there is no way men want to get near it and really the only acting required is a little itch itch.

Here are some excuses that you might want to stay away from:

Honey, there is this weird bump on my vagina.

Sorry, honey, I haven't taken a bath all week.

Oh no, I think I left a tampon up there for the past three weeks. (That even grossed ME out.)

Most of these would work, but you do eventually want your husband to have sex with you again, so choose your excuses wisely. Now, some asshole out there reading this might think, Something must be wrong with her sexually. No, from every woman I talked to this is an absolutely NORMAL thing that happens in EVERY marriage. Unfortunately, most husbands don't know we go to this extent to get out of sex, but it's true.

So the next time your vagina feels closed for business, you can try the honest route and communicate why you're too tired for sex or make it easy on yourself and simply start scratching.

Potty Training

I've always found it fascinating how men are able to whip out their penis and pee in any parking lot or any available alleyway. For us babes out there it ain't so easy. I'm sure all of you have tried it at least once: the squat, the release, and then the horrid pee stream that shoots out in every direction, soaking your shoes. Then we're left there searching around for some kind of leaf to wipe with while the guys simply just shake "it" off. Yeah, I might have pee envy, but I'm still glad I don't have the meat and potatoes that they have to deal with every day.

Growing up in a house with three sisters and no brothers we never really had a problem walking into our bathroom at night and enjoying a sit-down. The toilet was always down, and there was never any pee on the seat. My dad even peed sitting down. I asked him why once and he said, "I don't know, it's just more comfortable to sit." I thought that was genius. Why not sit? Once they do, their penis is going to hang in the down direction anyway, so why not relax and enjoy? Well, I guess if the man was blessed with an extra-large dong it could possibly slump low enough to hit the water, but c'mon, most of our husbands are not built like a professional basketball player, if you know what I mean.

I also find it funny how men pee in urinals next to each other. They're constantly whipping out their penis in front of other guys. They say they don't look, but you know they take a peek once in a while to check out the competition. No wonder they get pee stage fright. Even when I was in the bathroom with John there would be a seven-second delay before he could turn on the hose. I guess if we women had to pee standing up in front of one another we would get stage fright too. I really can't imagine standing there and pulling out my vagina and peeing on a wall talking to the girl next to me about yesterday's *General Hospital* episode. Weird!

So needless to say, when I starting living with my boyfriends later on in life, I quickly experienced the annoyance of the toilet seat left up or, even worse, the surprise wet seat. There truly is nothing worse than sitting on a wet seat. Actually, I take that back. Sitting on an airport toilet seat you thought you dried off but had some surprise drops—that's worse. Some stranger's pee. But we're talking about our husband's pee. Still gross but not revolting.

I'm currently in the process of teaching my three-year-old how to pee in a toilet. I had him watch Dad a couple of times because like father, like son, right? It was working until I realized that I needed to potty-train John at the same time as my three-year-old. If he's gonna teach our son how to pee, you can be damn sure he's gonna teach him right. So now it's lift, point, AIM, fire—AIM being the optimal word here—and then shake, lid down, and flush. There, I just saved my son's future wife endless nights of falling into the bowl. Which I'm sure has happened to YOU too!! Now that's freaking gross!

So if you can't train your man to aim accurately or keep the lid down, simply open his car door and pee on his seat. Then he too can enjoy the excitement of surprise pee.

Get Naked and Naughty!

Once you've tried every sexual position that you feel comfortable trying, what's next? What do you do to spice things up? Because, let's face it, it gets to be pretty stale after a while. Like going to get your tires rotated but using the same screws over and over and over again. Let me begin with simple ideas to spice things up and then I'll get to the raunchy ideas. First things first, try talking dirty. If you're already saying stuff like "Oooh, I'm getting wet" and "F*ck me harder!" . . . you're off to an okay start. If you've never said anything like that and are completely repulsed, please don't read the rest of this chapter. I think there is a rerun of *The Sound of Music* playing on a cable channel somewhere, but if you're a curious, naughty little woman, keep reading!

After so many years sex gets old, so in order to spice things up you must investigate what secretly turns your man on. Simply ask him what fantasies he pictures. What fantasies would he love to see happen? And then run with it. You can't get jealous, though. We all have secret fantasies. Even though I picture myself rubbing my crotch all over George Clooney, I'm not going to jump him on the red carpet and actually do it. Like if your guy has a thing for Britney Spears . . . try bringing her into some scenario. While you're having sex with him, ask him what he would do if he came home from work and you and she were in bed together. THIS does NOT make you gay! It's just a fun fantasy scenario to get turned on by. The scenario itself doesn't turn me on most of the time; it's watching him get so aroused he can't control it, and I'm forced to scream "Penny Marshall, Penny Marshall!" just to keep him from popping the lid. Feel free to tell him some of your fantasies also. If it involves other people, use a celebrity name or just the word "guy" in it because God forbid you should accidentally bring up his best friend. BIG NO-NO!!!

Once you've mastered some really sexy dirty talk, it's time to take it to the next level. If you are willing and open, porn could be a real turn-on. Once again, if this offends you at all, I think *The Sound of Music* is still playing. All other naughty, curious women keep reading! The first time I saw a porno I was at my cousin's house. (Isn't it always at your cousin's house?) I think I was ten and I could NOT believe that a man was kissing the place where she goes pee pee. My cousin and I were screaming, vowing to never EVER let that happen. Now, of course, it doesn't happen enough. But anyway, as I got older and have gone through enough relationships, I've found that watching an occasional porno film can be fun. It's easy foreplay. The key for any beginner is to get a porno that has girls in it who are bigger and not as pretty as you. This way you don't feel insecure compared to some hot silicone porn star who can deep throat. Amateur porn would be a good start. There is no professional lighting and the girls are real people. I'm telling you, if you haven't ever watched one with your man, go out and get one to surprise him. It will turn him on so much he probably won't be able to get past the opening credits without losing his load. If you're too embarrassed to go to

a store, order one online. There's plenty of them out there.

My last little idea actually came from my best friend from Chicago. She and I planned a girls' trip to Las Vegas recently, and we were talking about sex—the good, the bad, and the ugly. She told me she left her husband something behind that he could enjoy while she was gone. Just to sort of spice things up. If you're NOT a celebrity, this is a really fun, sexy thing to do. She made her own little video for him—doing her own thing, if you know what I mean—and left the tape under his pillow. I personally thought that was a GENIUS idea. That's a perfect example of how to completely turn on your man and keep things spicy. It also makes a really cheap birthday present.

So the next time you feel bored in bed, tell your husband that you've got a new movie for him to watch. Pop in the tape and watch the excitement on his face as he watches you on TV performing circus tricks with your vibrator. I guarantee you'll turn him on more than any bimbo porn star ever could!

The Horoscope Addict

The first time I ever heard what horoscopes and fortune-telling was all about was when I was in the sixth grade. My mother answered my question about the supernatural and certain people's ability to tell the future by telling me it was all rubbish. She said only God knows the future, but every morning I would catch her reading her horoscope in the newspaper. She would get really excited about good ones and reject the bad ones by turning the page quickly, stating, "They're full of baloney." By the time I got to the eighth grade it became my morning ritual. Before I left for school, I would flip open the paper and then ask a question to the universe like "Will Gary try to get to second base with me after school?" The problem was, the horoscopes I read at age twelve never gave the adolescent answer I wanted to hear. It usually said, *A business venture will soon unfold and a promotion will be offered to you*. What could that possibly mean to a twelve-year-old who wanted to get felt up?

As the years went on, I kind of let it go. I went through puberty like every girl should, lost and confused. Then, when I was in my early twenties, fortune-telling came back into my life with a big bang. I was walking past one of those palm-reader shops with the big neon hand blinking in the window. I had just dropped out of college, was totally in debt, and was living back with my parents. I had nothing to lose and needed a little direction, so I opened the door, hoping for some wise soul to tell me I had a purpose in this lifetime other than being really good at curling my hair.

I walked in, sat down, and pulled out a crumpled ten-dollar bill. The bug-eyed gypsy woman laid out my tarot cards and began to interpret what my life's destiny was. She told me I was about to move out west and I was going to become famous. I started laughing because I had just gotten out of work, where I made Polish sausage in a butcher shop for eight hours a day. I still had the aroma of pig under my fingernails, and this woman had just said I was going to become famous. She continued to say things like, You will also become a writer and publish some books. I shook my head and told this foolish woman the only book I had ever read was *Green Eggs and Ham* and that I bought all of my college essays from "smart people" in school. I left feeling duped and ten dollars poorer.

About six months later, I was driving cross-country to Los Angeles. I was dragging a small U-Haul filled with my college futon and TV. I had completely forgotten what the fortune-teller had said to me until I crossed the California border. "Holy shit, could that crazy bitch be right?" I was moving out west in the hopes of doing anything other than making Polish sausage, but the idea of having any sort of success made me smile. Shit, I would have been happy as a Bob Barker beauty.

Surprisingly, things seemed to happen exactly as she predicted. The negative part of this is that I became a serious psychic addict. For years I would dig out the best psychics and swerve my car into any spot that had an opening in front of a psychic shop. Then I learned how to read tarot cards and was giving readings to my friends and I even crashed some chat rooms, pretending to be a psychic. If you ever got a reading from someone on the Internet in the years between 1995 and 1998, I can guarantee it was probably me. I would come home from work and be online until dawn reading people. If people had only known it was ME giving them advice they would probably have shit themselves. Eventually all this stuff came crashing down on me and bit me in the ass. I was going through a really bad relationship, and my career was just as lost and confused as I was. I decided to find the best-of-the-best tarot reader, who supposedly did Madonna in her pre-Kabbalah days, and beg her for a glimpse into something brighter along the way. My reading turned out to be awful!! She said my career was going to go into a slump, and the guy I was with was really bad for me and I needed to get out. She went on and on until I made her leave. I kept dismissing her as a bad psychic, but she turned out to be right. I kept doing my own tarot cards and getting the same answer no matter how I altered the question. Finally I told myself to let go of all this shit and figure out my own path. When people put negative things in your head and that's all you think about, it's inevitable that you're probably going to make it happen. I finally took control of my own life and started making things happen on my own. Once in a while I will still read my In Touch horoscope, but that's about it.

So if you ever feel like getting a glimpse into your future, think twice. Not only because you might hold on to any negative predictions and make them a reality but also because that fortune-teller could just be me!!!!

Is That a Lobster in Your Pants or Are You Just Happy to See Me?

We've all seen those commercials where a woman is walking through a grassy field wearing white and the wind is blowing wistfully through her hair. She is talking about not feeling as fresh as she could be. These commercials usually come on at the worst time. For instance, once when my dad came over for a visit we were sitting on the couch watching TV when this horrid commercial came on about douching. I can take any good tampon commercial, but this was just darn right embarrassing.

I remember when I was going through puberty and I asked my mom what a douche was because I'd heard some girls talking about it at school. She looked at me and replied in a strict Catholic mom tone, "Douches are for sluts."

She went on to tell me that women have their own cleansing machinery in the vagina, and that our period cleans things out down there. She said douches were probably invented by some guy who was looking to make money. Personally, I think they were created by some guy who was married to a stinky vagina and was desperate to clean things up, but I still got my mom's point of view. I guess that message stuck in my head pretty well because to this day I still have never douched.

That being said, I've still had those "not-so-fresh" days. It's really kind of embarrassing, especially if you have to go buy a cream for it. I usually make someone else go buy it for me because the last thing I want is to be recognized at the market the one day I'm buying medicine for a yeast infection. At least it comes over the counter now. Remember when you had to get a prescription from your doctor?

I asked my doctor why men don't get yeast infections. He said they get them in a different way. When a man has

a yeast imbalance he gets that toe fungus under the nail. I've seen guys with this before, and it totally grosses me out. I'd much rather smell like sushi for a day than have that toe growth that lasts almost a year.

My worst fear is having a problem down yonder and not knowing it's even there until my man's head pops up from below with a look of confusion. Frankly, I think they're brave for going down there on a good day.

So if you wake up with that not-so-fresh feeling, throw on a white flowing dress and find the nearest grassy field to run through. It seems to work for those women on TV.

Stop Checking Out My Man, Bitch!

Even when I was a little blond bird in eighth grade, my twelve-year-old boyfriend would get jealous if I put on my Maybelline clear lip gloss. It didn't even have a tint of color in it, yet jealousy poured through his veins and he begged me to take it off. Relationships that followed seemed to repeat this pattern of jealousy. Why do some men get jealous when their own woman looks sexy? I don't get it. There are some assholes out there who might tell their wife she needs to lose a few extra pounds, and when the wifey does shed the weight and starts wearing flattering clothes, the man then loses his mind, calling her a tease. We can't win.

It's human nature to want to protect the things that are "ours," but it crosses a line when it comes to getting jealous over a miniskirt. I wish men would start to realize that women don't dress for other men. When we get dressed up to go out, you can be sure that every woman is ramming through her closet, trying to figure out what the other women are going to be dressed like. Our husbands need to know that we don't care about turning on Snausages. All we want is to be hip showing off the new blouse we just got at the mall. And hoping no one else has it.

On the flip side, we women have our own color of jealousy that runs through our veins. The most obvious example is when our man looks at other women when we are with him. I've become more amused by it, but when I was pregnant with some pretty low self-esteem, it would kill me. It would actually drive me to tears. I've come to realize that men will ALWAYS look at other women. It's inevitable. Sometimes they're not even pretty. It just takes a skirt and a pair of heels. Walking past construction sites is a perfect example—anything with boobs will be gawked and cooed at.

So mild jealousy happens with most of us. When it

gets out of control, I think it's because there is an under-
lying lack of trust. Trust is crucial in any solid relationship.
If you don't have it in marriage, I highly suggest reevalu-
ating yours. The hard part about that word is that there is
no action that revolves around it. Trust is simply something you have to put in your heart and hope for the best.

We can trust our husbands all we want, but most
women still don't truly know what the hell goes on at
those goddamned bachelor parties in Vegas. Well, guess
what, ladies! You will now. I crashed one in Vegas recently, and I can't wait to tell you everything. It's pretty
shocking, so if you don't want to read this, move to the
next chapter. For those who need to know . . . here's what
I saw.

On the hotel floor where I was staying there was a
pretty rowdy group of boys having a bachelor party. I've
always wanted to know what really goes on and decided
to invite myself to the party. I figured they wouldn't mind
if "Jenny McCarthy" joined their festivities, and this way I
would get to see what I've always wanted to know—if
boys cheat!! I walked into the room and greeted the boys
with a big hello and saw about ten to twelve men on
couches with women naked upside down on their heads,
working for tips. Okay, that didn't really surprise me that
much. They looked shocked as shit when they saw me
standing at the door, and I said, "Oh, please don't mind

me. I love watching." That led to a load roar, and I knew I was part of the boys' club. After watching the strippers perform wrestling moves with each other and put vegetables up their butts the party slowly started to move toward the bedrooms. I wasn't really aware of this because I was talking to my girlfriend, who I dragged along. We soon realized we were the only ones left standing in the room. The party boys were all locked in the bedroom with the two strippers. So I knocked on the door and (surprise, surprise) they didn't want to let me in. Gee, I wonder why? But I was clever and used some chick magic words and they pulled me and my friend in. What I saw was something I always knew happened—I just didn't want to believe it would go as far as it did. Half the room was having sex with one girl on a chair and the other half was watching the best man give it to the other girl from behind. Needless to say, my girlfriend and I felt VERY uncomfortable by this point and excused ourselves from the party. I saw exactly what I was hoping I wouldn't see. Boys cheat. Not all boys. Some were just watching, but I think there are more cheaters out there than not.

I never did understand the women who are in denial about their men cheating. If your husband is gone most weekends and he smells like perfume, wake up! Now, on the other hand, I also know some women who cheat. We aren't all angels either, but I can tell you it doesn't happen as often as with men. I know about ten married men who cheat and I know one married woman who does. Either way it's still wrong. If you don't have trust in your partner, what's the point of being married?

So remember to wear that miniskirt if it makes you feel good. Just let him know that he has nothing to worry about. But just a little warning to your husbands from me: What happens in Vegas doesn't stay in Vegas, because I'll be watching!!!

Are We Our Parents?

I'm sure you've heard the saying "You married your father." I hate that phrase simply because it sounds gross, but the older I get the more I understand and agree with the meaning behind it.

My mother and father met in beauty school. This is what my dad did with his GI money after Vietnam. When I asked him, "Why beauty school?" he replied, "That's where the pretty girls were." My dad wasn't stupid. He definitely had the charm that would attract babes—but most important, the hottest babe in the school, my mom. My dad put a perm solution on an old woman's head and then left for lunch. My mom was always paying attention to what he was doing and noticed that this little grandma had the solution on her head for over an hour. So she quickly poured water over the lady's head and all of her hair fell out with the perm rods still attached. My dad walked into class with ketchup still on his upper lip from lunch and was kicked out of beauty school. That, of course, didn't stop them from pursuing their love.

Like most Irish Catholic couples couples back in the day, they started their family at a very young age. I still think the reason was that celibacy was a real thing back then, and if men didn't force themselves to walk down the aisle they would have died of blue balls. Marriage for men meant sex, and they were excited for it. So excited that their wives spat out children, at least one child every two years. There are four girls in my family, and we are all two years apart. I would definitely say my parents got it ON.

As the years went by, my childhood seemed almost perfect. I had friends on the block to play with, my dad would come home from work and hug us and even coach some of our softball leagues, and my mom was our lunch mom at school. My sisters and I always felt safe and loved. My parents seemed to be doing everything right. However, behind closed doors, things sometimes weren't as shiny as they might have appeared. My parents fought on occasion—no hitting, but loud angry fights.

The negative thing I copied from my parents' marriage was the ability to brush things under the carpet. When the storm was over my mom quickly shoved it under the rug so her baby girls could see that today was a brand-new day and it was all behind us now. Yeah, until . . . the next time. We never really dealt with anything.

My sister would watch the *Brady Bunch* episodes and ask if we could have *Brady Bunch* meetings like they did. Now, I think that was the most genius thing ever. There should be Brady Bunch family meetings once a week in every home to put the shit on the table and deal with it. I still fight by running from the situation rather than by dealing with it. I'm slowly getting better, but it's still gonna be a while.

My parents wound up divorcing when I was twenty-one. I was sad for probably a week until I realized how much more happiness came into the family when they went their separate ways. I think they stayed together for the children longer than if there hadn't been any. I think that is the wrong thing to do. Children aren't stupid. They feel negativity and pick up bad traits, especially when

Mom is hiding the yucky to make everything appear to be great.

If you haven't taken an honest look at your own parents' relationship and how it affected you, I highly suggest doing so. You might be surprised to see that you have picked up some things along the way that are holding you back from making your home life the best it can be.

Honey, Would You Mind Picking Up My Breasts? They Fell Off the Bed Again

I hate that men age sexy! It's so unfair. They get that salt-and-pepper hair, and the crow's-feet around their eyes make them look more rugged. Like a cowboy. I dated an older guy when I was twenty-one. He looked really good for his age, and he kept up with my young energetic self. But even with all that, he was still old. He would listen to the oldies station and wore comfortable shoes. When your man starts buying clothes just because they're comfortable, you're in trouble.

One thing I always wondered about was whether or not your pubic hair turns gray. It's got to. Okay, I just called my mom and asked her if that happens and she said yes. But she made it clear to me that it hasn't happened to her yet. That seems crazy to me. Can you dye it if you hate it? And what happens to your vagina? Does that age, too? Is that why grannies wear granny panties? Because their vaginas now need extra support? And what about dryness? Holy shit. I'm scaring myself. I'm going to call my mom again.

Don't even get me started on boobs. Since I had my baby, they've headed south of the border. I used to do the pencil test. I would put a pencil under my boobs and they were so perky the pencil had nowhere to rest. Now I can stick a toaster under my boob and you wouldn't be able to find it. Recently I noticed a couple of hairs on my nipple. What the hell is up with that? And I swear to God I haven't had sex without wearing a bra in the past three years. The one time I didn't wear a bra my boobs got sort of soupy and slithered past my arms. They didn't bounce around like they do in porno—they just looked like pancakes being angrily slapped.

Face-lifts are something I'm all for. I would love to say that I think I'm going to grow old gracefully like Lauren Bacall, but I know I'm not. I'm going to end up looking like Joan Rivers with bigger boobs. I've been getting BOTOX in my forehead and I kind of dig it. I had to stop getting it around my eyes, though, because the area was so frozen that in pictures it looked like I had smelled a bad fart instead of smiling. I think if I lived in a city other than Los Angeles I wouldn't care as much about aging, but when you constantly see older men leaving their wives for twenty-year-old "poontango" you care.

Which brings me to the major change that men go through . . . THE MIDLIFE CRISIS. I've recently renamed it the "Tom Cruise Crisis" after I saw the infamous *Oprah* episode and Tom express his desire for twenty-year-old girls. Tom's midlife crisis proved to be the biggest public display of one we've seen in a while. I've heard that it starts with your husband caring more about his appearance. All of a sudden you will catch him out of the corner of your eye staring at himself in the mirror. He might even start using face products and toners for his skin. He might change his style of clothes because it looks "cooler." This is also the time he might want to trade in the SUV for a sports car. In L.A., for some reason, it's the Ferrari. IT'S SO STUPID. I just want to scream out the window, "WE ALL KNOW YOU HAVE GRAY PUBIC HAIR!"

Try not to make fun of your guy during this time. If you need to laugh, go in the pantry and let out a good chuckle. If he really wants a car during his "Tom Cruise

Crisis," let him get it. I would much rather have my husband get inside a sports car than get inside a twenty-year-old's "poontango."

Now, if God makes women go through the saggy boob experience as we age, at least He gave men the saggy balls experience. You know you might have to tell him to start wearing tighty whities if you're having sex and his saggy balls start flying through the air, hitting your body while you're doing it. And why do men's noses get bigger and why does hair start growing out of their ears? Screw the saying that he's got potatoes in his ears—he's got a freaking front lawn. It might be time for the Sharper Image nose-and-ear-hair clippers for Christmas. GROSS!

The bittersweetness in aging is that you and your guy can go through it together. You can look at each other's faces and see the years and memories that surround every wrinkle. I just hope someday down the road, instead of turning into Joan Rivers, I'll be able to look past my cracking skin and thick toenails and see the cute Jenny I was when I was twenty-five. Yeah, right, this is L.A. My husband will be in a yellow Ferrari, and I'll be at my hairdresser's dyeing my pubes. Hey, there is nothing wrong with dreaming!

The Seven-Year Itch

I used to think the Seven-Year Itch was a myth or for old people who didn't know how to live it up or for couples who maybe never had the magic to begin with. That is, of course, until I was going on my seventh year of marriage. One morning I rolled over in bed and saw a nose with hair sticking out that was snoring with some pretty bad morning breath. That was the day I began to itch.

I've talked to other couples who have confirmed this

as a real thing. It's almost like a virus: You either fight it and get past it or die with the rest of the bacteria. God, I wish there was a cream for it. Rub it on and your marriage becomes shiny and new again.

Marriage is a pretty amazing thing when you think about it. For two people to live together for so long under the same roof is a big accomplishment. Fifty-year anniversaries are becoming extinct, yet again proving that long marriages deserve awards and praise. Sometimes I see old people in restaurants sitting together eating their meals and I watch them. Sometimes it makes me sad. They don't even talk. Is it because they have nothing else to say, or can they simply read each other's mind by now? I wonder if, forty-three years ago, their Seven-Year Itch went untreated and they stayed together despite their itchiness.

The good news is, I have seen really old couples who still hold hands, not just to help each other walk but because they really want to. I love seeing that. It gives me such great hope. Those are the couples who found the medicine for their itch and managed to move forward. But how? When I close my eyes I can definitely see me with some old fart sitting at a restaurant drooling at each other. It makes me giggle and at the same time it makes me scared. I so desperately don't want to be in a marriage that starts to feel like a brother-and-sister relationship. You know what I mean? I want love, sex, excitement for years to come.

I think the medicine for the itch comes with time. Something happens that ignites the fire again even if it goes out quicker than you had hoped. At least you can see it working. The memories you both share together in your lifetime, like watching your baby's first steps, watching him stare at you naked out of the corner of your eye, are all things you shouldn't take for granted. Let those moments touch you again and then maybe you can see through new eyes. Because, really, that's all it is—looking at things from a new perspective. My girlfriend said she so desperately wanted to look at her husband again and say, "God, it's so cute the way he . . ." It had been a while since she'd said anything like that because, after so many years, all those cute things turned into annoying things. Which is completely normal in my eyes. When you co-habitate long enough, you get used to shit. So she desperately wanted to fill in the blank. "God, it's so cute the way he . . . ?" So one day, she decided to eavesdrop on her husband taking a shower. He was doing a dance as he was scrubbing his butt cheeks. She said it wasn't sexy, by any means, but it was really cute. CUTE! There it was. She said to me, "God, it's so cute the way he scrubs his butt

cheeks." She was so excited to fill in her blank. She said even though it was something as simple as that, it made her smile to know that her man has a cute butt-scrubbing dance.

Now, if your itch is very bad and you can't find a cream for it, maybe it's time to reexamine the relationship. Sometimes I think marriage licenses should be like driver's licenses. They expire after a number of years, and in order to keep going you have to renew. Wouldn't that be kind of genius? It would force you both to look at the relationship, and if it's not working, the marriage would expire so you could go on your merry way, or on the positive side of it, you could look at each other and say we really want to renew. What a way to keep it fresh!!

So, as the years progress, don't forget to pay attention to the little things that do make you smile. Those are the creams you'll need to keep that itch under control for years to come!

Bleaching Your Asshole??

What is the world coming to? Even I was shocked when I heard that the latest new thing going on was to bleach your asshole. If you live in small-town U.S.A. and you're completely repulsed, just wait. L.A. starts these weird things and then in about five years it will be available at your local bank after a nice deposit.

I didn't really understand why a girl would need to do this. Yes, large logs do pass through, but doesn't toilet paper do the job of cleaning things up? I was informed by women who have had this procedure done that a girl wouldn't bleach it for sanitary reasons, but because some people have a darker circle around that area. This was totally new to me because I had never really checked mine out. I mean, I've stopped in the mirror to squeeze my fat or look at some cellulite, but to bend over and spread the cheeks to see how things look in the asshole department? I don't think so.

Later that week I was having sex with John and was reminded about the topic as he flipped me over into the doggy-style position. I couldn't help but wonder if he was looking down into a dark donut around my butt hole. So I faked a few orgasms, got him to the finish line, and then plopped down. I was dying to ask him but didn't know how. I finally just said it the only way I could.

"Do I have ring around the asshole?"

He looked at me weirdly and replied with, "Do you mean that dark circle around your ass?"

I leaped off the bed and started screaming and flailing around the room.

"What do you mean, that dark circle around my ass? Is there really one there?"

I couldn't believe he'd replied so quickly and confidently about it. "Yes, there is."

I started screaming and flailing around the room again. "How come you never told me?"

He replied with "Because I like your ass no matter what."

I said, "Do YOU have ring around the asshole?"

He said, "I don't think so."

With that cocky response I made him stand up, bend over, and spread 'em. I couldn't believe my eyes. He had a perfect butt hole! Not even a dingleberry. I charged into my bathroom, turned on all the overhead lighting, bent over, and spread 'em!

"DAMN IT!!!"

He was right. I started to call my friends and ask them if they had this also. Half did and half didn't and a few of them were so weirded out that I still haven't heard back from them. I know it's not the end of the world, but it freaks me out when I hear or find out something that I knew nothing about and then realize I've been living with this ring-around-the-asshole for thirty-three years.

Now, what's a girl to do? I'm still embarrassed to go to the gyno, let alone go to the nail salon and ask for some ass bleaching. After about five minutes of really considering it, I let go of the dream of the perfect asshole. I figured after blowing out my vagina from childbirth those

ailments far outweigh the other. And if any guy has a problem with my loose vagina and C-section scar, then he can kiss my ring-around-the-asshole!

So go ahead and check out yours. You know you were going to after reading this anyway. And if you turn out to be one of the unlucky ones, don't fret. Just know that you're got a famous friend in Hollywood who has the same ring-around-the-asshole as you.

To Shave His Balls or Not to Shave His Balls

All right, if we women have to keep up with the times by bleaching our asses, then the men can get down and do a little upkeep themselves. Ryan Seacrest started the metrosexual trend and it's taken off more than I ever thought it would. College boys began feeling the need to get manicures and pedicures, and I knew at that moment we were headed into a new era. The "can-I-borrow-your-hair-gel?" man!

The one nice thing about this new trend is that men can relate now to some of what women have to go through to maintain their appearance.

There are a couple of negative side effects that do come with a well-groomed man. One is the fact that now he takes longer than you do to get ready. It's amazing that women can make dinner, take a shower, put the baby to bed, and be in a dress with an updo standing at the front door and our men are still coiffing their hair in the mirror. This is the perfect example again of how we can multitask yet men can't. . . . resulting in the Mr. Potato Head syndrome!

The other negative side effect is his using up all of your products. I remember walking into the bedroom and seeing John with a mud mask on his face. Then there's not being able to find your stuff because men never put things back where they find them.

"Where the hell are my tweezers?"

He replies, "I had an ingrown pubic hair."

Ew, gross!

Although I must say I am glad that men have started to groom down below, and if your man hasn't ever done it, I encourage you to get him to try. Men's pubes can really grow out of control, especially if you have a hairy man. The guys who have a carpet that starts at their neck and ends far south of the border need to groom the carpet once it grows past the belly button. It needs to feel like we are entering a different room when we go down there. Take us from the shag carpet to at least a throw rug. If they don't, by the time we hit the meat and potatoes we're coughing up fur balls. If he owns an electric razor, tell him to set it at number two. It seems to be the perfect length.

Now let's move down a little farther. To the balls! I thought it was a little, um . . . not right for guys to shave their balls UNTIL I ventured down there and was pleasantly surprised. I liked it. I really liked it. It was smooth and because they were now hairless, there was no cheesy odor that sometimes accumulates down there. And men say that it gives them extra sensitivity. A definite thumbs-up.

I would highly recommend having your man avoid waxing at all costs. Men can't handle that kind of pain on their elbows, let alone their balls. If stubble starts to bother him from shaving, simply lie and tell him how that turns you on as much as his bald balls.

So if you're not sure what to get your man for Christmas, keep in mind getting him a nice razor. Tell him that you're really in the mood this year to suck on some smooth jingle balls. If he doesn't want to try it, let your own lawn grow out for a while. Let's see how well he does. I guarantee it will get him hummin' your tune!

Don't You Know Me by Now?

This one just kills me. You'd think that after being with us for such a long period of time our men would know us completely inside and out. I bet some of your men don't even know what color your eyes are. It's mind-boggling to me that men have the ability to either tune us out or simply ignore the details that make up our likes and dislikes.

A perfect example of this is gift buying. It's pretty

good in the beginning of the relationship. You'll get jewelry or a nice leather coat. Then once you take your vows, he starts buying you earrings with peacocks hanging off them. "Oh, wow, honey, these are so much better than that zebra necklace you got me last year."

Whenever my birthday was approaching I got nervous. I begged John just to spend the money on a nice dinner and not to buy me anything. Of course that never happened. After dinner he would pull out a box and I would be hoping to God I didn't have to fake this one. I would slowly unwrap the gift and usually force a pretty good smile. On one occasion I pulled out a deck of . . . "magic cards."

He said, "You didn't want me to spend a lot of money, so I thought you might want to learn some magic."

Learn some magic? What the hell was he thinking? Sure, let me put my son to bed, load the dishwasher, and then read my book of magic tricks to learn the craft before I go to sleep every night.

It also amazes me that when men try to buy us clothes it's usually something we would never wear. I was always worried when I pulled something out of the box. "Is this how people see me? In a sweater vest with hearts on it?" Every day I wore the same sweats over and over again. What made him choose this?

He said, "You should expand your wardrobe."

"So I can look like a dork?" I replied.

Besides taste, I don't think men comprehend sizes. I'm sure some husbands still don't know their wife's size. They go shopping and find a saleswoman who fits their wife's build and ask her to either try the item on or hold it up to her. John would buy me things that weren't even close to my size and he'd explain, "Well, that's all they had left."

So what part of my ass cheek does he think is possibly going to fit into a size 2?

Another great gift-buying fiasco is when your man buys you lingerie as a gift. I'm not talking about a beautiful bra and panties, because that would be nice. I'm talking about sexy lingerie you can't wear under your clothes. The ones made strictly for sex. This is NOT a gift for us. It's a gift for THEM. It's not like I'm going to run to my drawer at night to put on my crotchless underwear because I enjoy the nighttime breeze. It drives me mad. And they're not even comfortable or flattering. Just keep the tags on and return them for some pretty undies, and when he asks you to put on the naughty ones he got you, just say, "I'd rather be naked, honey." That response should work every time.

Last but not least is the food buying. John would come

home from the store and tell me he bought me my favorite candy bar and then pulls out a Twix. In the seven years I was married, I had never even said the word *Twix*. And I swear to God when I tell you this happened at least five more times with the same freakin' Twix bar until I finally shouted the word *RAISINETS!!!!!!* He then came home with three boxes of them anytime he went to the store.

Coming home with takeout was another fun surprise. He'd pull out a breaded chicken sandwich, telling me I was going to love this, when I hadn't eaten chicken in ten years because I hate the taste of it. I just stood there with this look of awe on my face as he sank his teeth into the burger I wanted.

Even though this is all trivial crap, it's still funny to watch the person who is supposed to know you better then anyone buy you the rainbow-colored coat you never would wear in a million years. But like they say, it's the thought that counts, right? Um . . . only if the tags are still on it.

The Back Door Is Closed

Let's face it, there are only so many sexual positions out there to choose from. And lately I feel like you have to pay me to be the one on top. It's a lot of work! I'm not very good at it, and after having a baby, I find being on top can cause serious injury to self-esteem. It looks like somebody grabbed my nipples and pulled them to the other side of the room and let go! So if I'm bouncing around on top, the things my boobs are doing are absolutely embarrassing. When I was younger I used to hear older wives talk about how they kept the lights off during sex. I never understood that when I was a dumb twenty-two-year-old girl. NOW I GET IT!!! If a light is ever turned on while I am naked I started screaming. High-pitched shrieks shake the walls of my house to make the f*cking light disappear as quickly as possible.

Let's slide right into a different position now. The doggy-style position. Most guys like it because it's different and your ass is smiling right at him while in a vulnerable position. As I got older, I noticed that men started to enjoy touching my back door. I always considered my back door to be an EXIT, not an entrance. But for some reason men like to find their way there. I don't get it. Don't they care that it's a poop chute? I think for them it's kinky and much tighter, so they are drawn to it. I've heard guys say that when they were very young, like nine, they used to stick their penis into anything that had a hole in it, a Jacuzzi jet, a toilet paper roll hole, anything that they could fit their penis into. It doesn't surprise me then when they eventually ask to play with the back door.

Guys also like having their own back door played with. Personally, I have a problem playing with the back door. I had an ex pull out a tub of Vaseline once during sex and when I asked, "What the hell is that for?" he smiled and replied, "For your finger."

EWW!!!!! Gross. Go clean out your own backyard!

There are some women who are actually into it. My girlfriend is one of them. When I asked her about it, she said it's kind of kinky for her, too. Sometimes she likes it, but she has to be really warmed up. She also said when she agrees to it she usually gets whatever she wants for about a month.

Being a curious sexual person myself I have indeed tried it for the sake of spicing things up, and I gotta tell ya, I freakin' hated it. Thank God I'd had a few drinks 'cause it probably would've hurt a lot more than usual. I toughed it out and then screamed to get it out. It lasted all of about thirty seconds, and I'm proud to say my back door has been closed ever since.

If you are ever going to let your man visit your "dark side of the moon," be sure he wipes off his penis before he re-enters your vagina. If not, you will have the worst bladder infection you've ever had in your life.

So you can either be like me and permanently leave your back door as an exit only or be the brave soul who leaves it open, awaiting the eager dragon that is so desperate to get inside. Ouch!

Please Don't Make Us Go to YOUR Mother's House for Christmas Again!!

O h, the holidays! Every year families come together from near and far to join in a celebration
of love and unity. They share stories and give thanks for
all the beautiful blessings that have come into their lives,
and they spread goodwill for one another's future. If this
at all resembles you and your family, I would say you are
on crack. Don't get me wrong, I love holidays, I just don't
like the drama that usually comes with them.

When you're little it's amazing how oblivious you are to the politics that go on with the adults. All I cared about was what Santa was going to bring and if there was enough Jell-O for me to gorge on after dinner. Little did I know that my mother and aunts were watering down the men's drinks so they wouldn't become too intoxicated to drive the family home. I didn't know that half the family hated the other half and that they wanted to kill each other at the dinner table. I remember thinking that everyone has police cars showing up at Christmas to break up fights between drunken relatives. My little cousins and I used to shout, "Yay, the police cars came to our party again!" Oh yes, those were the innocent years.

If weirdness in your own family isn't already enough, you go and get yourself married and add another dimension of insanity to your life. If you get along with your new family tree, good for you. Some people aren't so lucky. The biggest problem could be figuring out whose house you're going to spend the holidays at. Is it his mom's for Thanksgiving and your mom's for Christmas? I think I would rather get two extra Pap smears a year than have to figure out whose house we are going to for the holidays. Once you have kids I think it should be a law that everyone comes to you. If there are many kids on each side of the family, then it should be the house with the youngest baby. It should also include everyone else cleaning up because the duties of a new mom are much more important than dishwashing.

Traveling with children during the holidays is truly hell on earth. No one gives you sympathy in airports when you're hauling your child through terminals. They tend to look at you as if you're diseased or like you just shat in their Cheerios. People are honestly happier to see a dog board the plane. "Oh, look at the cute shih tzu. What a pretty dog you have." Then comes the family with children boarding the plane. The first-class passengers whisper to one another, "Thank God those dirty brats are sitting in coach."

Even if you get the luxury of winning Christmas on your side of the family versus your husband's, you still have to deal with another holiday downer. . . . your own bad blood. There is always ONE embarrassing family member. We have a nutbag in our family who brings up shit that happened to us when we were in third grade.

I would say, "Can you pass the gravy?"

She would reply, "Why should I? You wore my brand-new gym shoes in high school without telling me and stepped in dog poo and lied to me about who did it."

I would just stare in awe that at thirty-three years old I had to hear my childhood mistakes being compared to turkey gravy. Unfortunately, issues like this come up all the time during holidays because people haven't worked

past their own shit or childhood dramas and feel the need to remind you of their pain at every holiday. Even your own parents, who might be stuck in their old-fashioned upbringing, can bring you down by telling you things you don't want to hear anymore. "Yes, Mom, I'm quite aware that Jesus died so we could all be here today to eat this dead bird."

So the next time your relatives try to force you to come to their house for the holidays, simply be honest and let them know that you were really looking forward to having it on your own. If that doesn't work, tough it out the only way I know how: "Can we add some more rum to this eggnog?"

What Happened, Jenny?

I think you've all come to realize by now that I'm very
honest and truthful about everything in my life. I
couldn't finish this book and not write about what happened with my own marriage. Most celebrities think personal matters should remain private, but after writing a
chapter on trying "back door sex," how could I not be
honest about my own breakup?

This book was originally titled *Marriage Laughs.*

When I began writing, I was having a really great time breaking the code of silence about the things women have to experience in marriage. As I was writing it, the book started to become very *Oprah* journal-like. Soon I started to struggle when it came to writing things that were loving and caring about my husband. I would write a chapter and then look at it and say, "Holy shit, I'm lying to my readers." I closed my computer and cried really hard. And couldn't stop crying. I realized at that moment I couldn't brush my shit under the carpet anymore and hope things would change. As I lay on my bed with my computer yelling at me because the battery was dying, I dug deep into my soul. I wanted to figure out what went wrong.

The day I met John, I told him I was going to marry him. Literally. Two weeks later I was engaged, and we got married six months later. We seemed to be so similar in so many ways, but something was always a little off. I kept telling myself that no one is perfect and to just deal with it. We were always very respectful of each other and had great sex, yet in my heart something felt sad. I couldn't figure what it was. There wasn't an actual problem I could point to and say, "Hey, could you fix this?" I was so confused. So I put myself back in time to the beginning of our relationship. It then became obvious to me . . . after a few therapy sessions. I married a man I never got to know. I created an absolute fantasy of who I thought this man was, and all these years he couldn't live up to that fantasy. Most of the time I blamed him for doing things wrong because in my head my fantasy man would NEVER do that. I realized I didn't fall in love with John, I fell in love with the fantasy of who I hoped he was.

I knew I had just had a very big Oprah lightbulb moment. The question I had for myself now was, Do I tough it out for the sake of my kid? Or do I set myself free and hope that I can find love and allow John to find someone who loves him for himself? My mom and dad stayed together for thirty years for the sake of my sisters and me. Growing up in that environment made it obvious to me that I should not repeat that cycle. I knew what had to be done.

I was driving in the car with John one morning and looked at him and sadly said, "I want a divorce." The look on his face, needless to say, was utter shock. He kept pleading, "Why?" I asked him if he was truly happy also. He took a moment and replied, "No." We both cried and talked at the side of the road for a few hours. We talked about trying to save us but knew it was too late. We had needed to save us seven years ago by really getting to know who we were.

Believe it or not, we had a truly amicable divorce. We realize we're much better friends than we were a married couple and even better parents because we are both happy. He comes over every day to put our son to bed, and I love that I can say he is now one of my best friends and an even better dad to our son.

We might not have beat the odds in the Hollywood, where "dreams" come true, but at least I can say I followed my heart, and that's where I expect all my dreams to finally come true.

The Juggling Mom

Ever since I was a little girl I have had a problem with learning how to juggle. I would throw the balls up in the air and whisk my little hands around trying to catch them as they fell. As an adult the only balls I learned how to juggle were my husband's. Now that those balls are gone, I'm constantly dodging the rest of life's incredibly large balls.

How do women do it? I still don't know. I find myself

bursting into tears while I'm trying to do laundry, talk on the phone, make chicken nuggets, and change a diaper in the same breath. If God had made us like octopuses I could see how we could get a lot more done. But God didn't. We are expected to uphold the same traditions from "back in the day" yet still bring home a paycheck. If you are a working mom, you give everything to your job when you are there. Then when you get home you give everything to your kids. By the time you tuck them into bed you have no energy left to satisfy your husband's throbbing dragon. There just doesn't seem to be enough time in the day . . . EVER! I was trying to think of a comparison so a man could truly understand, and the only thing I came up with is telling him to imagine having to run one mile in thirty seconds. He would reply, "It's impossible. I need more time." I would then say, "There is no more time. That's all ya got. And while you are trying to make it to the finish line, whip up a pot roast, feed the dogs, wash the baby, and load the dishwasher—all in thirty seconds." That's honestly what it feels like.

I have had the experience of being both a working mom and a stay-at-home mom since my son was born, so I can at least give an honest and accurate account of the pros and cons of each. I work sometimes for a month straight and then I'm home for three months. To this day I have never had a nanny in this house while I'm not working. So if I say I'm cleaning up my son's poo-poo diapers while vacuuming, it's true.

I found that stay-at-home moms and working moms both have their ups and downs. The advantage of being at work is that you actually get to sit down for an hour at lunch. There is no screaming going on, and you can actually hear yourself think. It's also very rewarding to be told you are good at something, because unfortunately you won't hear too much praise from your kids till they leave for college. The cons of being a working mom include watching that cute face stare at you through the front door mouthing "MAMA, come back!" every morning. Also, your weekends are not days off for you. Saturdays and Sundays are catch-up days for buying food and diapers you couldn't get all week.

The biggest pro about being a stay-at-home mom is that YOU are the one raising your kids. You don't miss out on all the milestones someone else would have probably seen first. The cons I personally found were looking like a house rag most of the day, because why bother making myself look good while I'm watching my baby? The other con is only having your baby to talk to all day long. I only wish my son was able to have a conversation about the *Oprah* episode I was forcing him to watch. He would only make comments about the diaper commercials in between the show.

Now that I'm a single mom, I feel like I'm only getting fifteen seconds to run a two-mile race. Less time and a longer distance. It's so incredibly hard at times that I think I'm going to break. At least when your husband is there you can say, "Hey, watch the baby for a second," while you lie down or even run to the store. I don't have that luxury. I can't take showers anymore because no one is watching him. So all of my washings are WITH him in the tub. I can't tell you the last time I took a bath without a rubber duckie or smelling like Monster Bubbles.

The most important thing I've learned in all this juggling is that it's quality, not quantity. I might not get all my shit done in one day, but at least I know I made my son giggle so hard it made ME pee in my pants. For generations to come I'm sure women will be juggling even more, but I have no doubt in my mind that we will make it work because some how, some way, we do make the impossible possible.

Jennyology

What I'm about to explain is simply my own personal take on spirituality. I'm not preaching or telling you that I'm right, so I don't want any letters from religious groups. It's just my own viewpoint on the matter.

I was raised in a VERY Catholic family on the South Side of Chicago. I have hundreds of relatives, some of whom are priests and nuns. I attended Catholic school my whole life and even went to an all-girl school . . . yuck. My whole childhood I grew up with Jesus pictures and statues that stared at my every move in the house. Needless to say, I was God-fearing. Every night before I went to bed, I would say sixty "Our Father" prayers, sixty "Hail Mary"'s, and sixty "Angel of God" prayers. Then I prayed for every dog in the neighborhood: Pickles, Pepper, Cookie, Kelly, Sheba, Woofie, and Penny. I even lay in bed with my Mother Mary statue and rosaries, praying to God that Satan wasn't going to enter my body while I was sleeping.

Throughout my entire childhood I lived in this kind of fear. Fear of burning in hell with the devil for an eternity. When I actually did "sin" I would race to the church to tell the priest why I broke a commandment. I had to make sure that before I went to bed that night my soul was clean just in case I died in my sleep.

It wasn't until I moved away from home that I started to let go of some of my fear. Not all of it, but enough of it to have fun in college and go to bed with a boy without my Mother Mary statue lying in between us. It was during this time that I started reading books on spirituality and forming my own views on why I am here. I started to look at my life and realized that when bad things happened because of something I did there was always a consequence. I didn't need to run to a priest—I just needed to look back at the situation and learn from my mistakes. Guilt about doing something wrong was getting me nowhere. So I stopped feeling so bad all the time and forgave MYSELF and looked at bad situations as lessons learned and tried not to repeat my mistakes.

When I moved out to Los Angeles, I received a couple of letters from my uncle, who is a priest, damning my soul to hell. He said I would amount to nothing and that I was evil in the eyes of God. I'm sure this is probably one of the reasons I worked my ass off in this town to prove him wrong and probably another reason why I'm so big and goofy on television. I was so tired of being locked in a box of can't-dos and can-dos that I just wanted to express myself and try to make people laugh. If wanting to make people laugh as a career choice is evil, then I'm gonna have a good time burning in hell with some pretty famous people.

"Hey, Lucy, your ass is on fire."

"Thanks, Jenny, you're pretty 'hot' yourself."

I feel so much more secure with my faith now by having my own spiritual viewpoint about it and not being bogged down memorizing gospels in school. I'm a better person today knowing that I choose what I do in this lifetime and that I'm going to be the one responsible for my actions and I will suffer the consequences on a daily basis, not necessarily by burning in flames for all of eternity.

Life feels like a big school to me now. You get beat up, but you pick yourself back up and try to move to the head of the class without stepping on or hurting anyone along the way. Unless, of course, they stepped on you first; then beat the shit out of them and move on. I'm kidding.

So no matter what religion you are, I think having faith in something higher and for the greater good can help you get through the hardest school you've ever been through . . . life. Except if you're an atheist. Then you're going to die a horrible death . . . just kidding.

Faking It

J ust writing the title of this chapter makes me smile because I know that most women, if not all women in
the world, fake orgasms. If you say you've never faked
them, either your guy is standing right next to you or
you're a big fat liar. And if your guy asks you if you ever
have, I'm sure you've replied the same way I have: "Not
with YOU, honey."

Before I divulge all of my faking-it stories, I would first

like to bitch about why women were NOT built with the same horniness as men. It's so unfair. Since we do most of the work to maintain the human race, you would think God would make it a fair game. I work all day, stop at the store, pick up groceries, feed the baby, clean the house, put the baby to bed, and my body is just supposed to be "randy" for my man? That's funny. That's really funny.

And how can men's dicks get hard at such inappropriate times? I would bet a million dollars that if I went to a funeral and asked my man if he wanted to go into the bathroom for a quickie he would have to limp the whole way to the restroom covering up his immediate hard-on. I, on the other hand, get horny four days a month—two days before my period and two days after my period. That's it!! Can I be worked up to a horny place instead of waiting for those four days each month? SURE. But the older and busier women get, the more warming up we need. And most of the time a husband's idea of foreplay is him pulling his dick out of his pants.

When you first learn about orgasms as a young girl you learn about two different kinds, the "inner" and the "outer." Both can be faked quite easily, but all women would obviously prefer not to. The outer one, known as the clitoral orgasm, is much, much easier to have. I have no idea why this is. It's a very rare occasion when I have had to fake these, unless the exes in the past were trying desperately to find the spot and got lost at the deli counter.

The internal orgasm, known as a vaginal orgasm, is much harder to achieve. For years I thought these were myths. I couldn't understand what all the fuss was about. I thought for sure I was born without a G-spot. I faked these for YEARS. (Sorry to all the exes in the past. It's true.) Almost ALL women I talk to have yet to even have an internal orgasm. So if you're one of them, don't be alarmed. Most said the only way they can get off is by working the outside while he's inside. I finally had success when I met the right guy and he moved me into positions that worked. Most men aren't that giving or talented, though, so if your guy is not one of them, you're not alone.

As I'm sure most of you know, orgasms require deep concentration. If you are at all distracted, like thinking about what groceries you need, you probably won't be able to get to the finish line. It's amazing to me how much brain work it takes for a girl to have an orgasm. Guys just need to look at a nipple and they lose it. Unfortunately, after childbirth and gravity, I don't think my nipples are as alluring as they used to be. They're starting to resemble elbows.

The most common reason why we women fake orgasm is to help our man get off so we can be done with sex. If it's taking too long and you just want it to be over so you can watch TV, you shout a little oooh ahhh and pop goes the weasel . . . he's done.

A second reason for faking is that you just don't feel like concentrating so hard to reach an orgasm, but he's already gone down under and is trying his hardest, so you shout a little oooh ahhh to reward him for a job well done.

Another reason to fake is that you want to look hot and sexy during sex. Let's face it, if we didn't fake it, half the time we might look like dead fishes just laying there. Shouting a little oooh ahhh can make you look like a good lay.

The last reason why a woman would fake an orgasm is because HE HAS NO IDEA WHAT HE IS DOING. If a man sucks at it, you have no choice but to fake it!

But if you encourage your man into doing it the way you like it, you just might get away with faking a few less orgasms. Tell him it's a delicate flower down there and that it needs to be teased. A nice rhythmic motion is always good, and if he avoids using his teeth, even better. Tell him even though it looks like bologna, it's not. Don't chew it!

The one good thing in all this is that men have no

idea if an orgasm is fake or not. So there really isn't any way to get busted. One good tip, if you're not already doing it, is to squeeze your vagina muscles during your oooh and ahhh shouts. It puts the cherry on a really great performance!

The Mommy Hangover

My first experience drinking was in the attic of my girlfriend's house back on the South Side of Chicago. There was a group of us, including some boys, and we were breaking into my friend's grandma's imported vodka cabinet. The whole neighborhood I lived in was Polish, and those Polish folks really loved their vodka. The labels on the bottles even looked homemade. It was all in Polish, but I knew the one with the exclamation mark must've meant it was really strong, so we broke it open. There was a boy in the group I really liked, and being the idiot I was, I wanted to show him how cool I could be and dared myself to chug half the bottle. Everyone responded with "No way, you won't be able to do it." Well, that was all I needed to hear. I was only a freshman in high school and weighed maybe 110 pounds, but I figured I had the blood of an Irishwoman and could handle it. With that, my idiot self chugged half the bottle of "Zschofski!!!" vodka. Ten minutes later I blacked out and faintly remember puking on everyone, including the boy I liked. People were screaming as vomit projectiled all over the attic including on my new Limited Forenza sweater and Z. Cavaricci pants (remember those?). My friends finally got me home and told my mom I had food poisoning. I remember throwing up for two days and swearing to God that I would never drink again if He could just make it all go away. Cut to . . . me in my freshman year in college on my knees throwing up and praying to God that if He just makes it go away I will never drink again. I think God should really tune us out or hit the mute button when He hears the cries from us earthlings every weekend. Save the prayers for the really big stuff, not just when we're on our knees praying in front of a toilet.

The only good thing about drinking back in our

youngster days was the nonexistent hangovers on a non-bingeing night. I could drink pretty heavily in college, puke my brains out, and still be able to make my eight A.M. history class feeling pretty good. Then age kicks in and you wake up and realize it's not as easy as it used to be. Your hangover would last till at least five P.M. the next day, and that's only if you were able to get a big, fat cheeseburger down to soak it all up. Thank God I lived it up in college because once you become a mom . . . things change.

The first two and half years after my son was born I never even got tipsy. I was so tired from being a mom all day that the idea of having a drink sounded exhausting. I hardly wanted to go out at all, but my friends were yelling at me for years to have a girls' night out, so I finally weakened and did it. I gotta tell ya, I'm glad I did. I had the best time ever! We laughed, we told stories, we were dancing like idiots, we peed on the side of the street, we did everything we could to feel like girls again and not diaper-changing moms. On my way home I thought about the importance of friendship and how I really needed to see my friends more often. I climbed into my bed, burped a couple of times, and then smiled at the ceiling while I was watching it spin as it did back in the college days. My eyes finally settled and I closed them peacefully. Seconds later, I heard . . .

"Mama?"

My eyes popped open in horror.

"Oh NO!"

I looked at the clock and realized it was time for my son to get up. I couldn't comprehend how I was physically going to go from fun girlfriend back to mom in less than thirty seconds. But if you're a mom, you know that somehow you always seem to rise to the occasion. And that's exactly what I did. Well, sort of. I rose to my feet and went into his room and said, "Good morning, buddy, you wanna watch *Teletubbies*?"

His eyes lit up like I was offering him the world because usually I don't let him watch those freaky stuffed aliens that have satellite televisions in their stomachs.

"Yes, *Teletubbies*!" he shouted.

So we climbed into my big bed and turned on *Teletubbies*. I snuggled close and was grateful to those freaky aliens for granting me rest after my one fun night out.

Unfortunately, what felt like seconds later, the Teletubbies were shouting their good-byes and I knew what had to be done. I lifted up my head and looked at his cute face and said, "Hey, you want to watch *Teletubbies* again?"

With that, I hit the Play button and caught at least another half hour of rest. I closed my eyes and was never so happy to fall asleep to "Uh-oh, Tinky Winky, uh-oh, Dipsy."

Who knew those little bastards could sound so good?

Even though that whole day was a struggle, I was glad I did it. I had fun with my friends. I think once every six months it should be a ritual. The next time, though, I think I will have the babysitter stick around the following morning. The last thing I want is for my son to start pretending to turn on his stomach TV and play with his head antennae. Otherwise Mommy might dip into a little Zschofski!!!! Uh-oh, Tinky Winky.

Life's Embarrassing Moments

Why is it that when we feel like we look really hot or on top of the world something happens that makes us fall to the ground? Walking into a party wearing that new dress that you know is better then any other bitch's dress and everyone turns to look at you when you walk in the room and you just stand there, thinking, Oh yeah, check this shit out, and then you fall down a flight of stairs. I know everyone has had at least one of these moments. I've been blessed with many. For what little dignity I have left after sharing all aspects of myself, I'm only going to share two with you. They are the worst and they will plague me until I die.

Back in the ancient year of 1993, I was on my way to Chicago to do an autograph signing. It was a red-eye flight, and I was desperate to get some sleep because as soon as I got off the plane I was being taken to a car convention to take pictures with horny men. I remember sweating the whole time on the plane while everyone else was bundled in blankets. I knew something was wrong. When the plane landed I could barely make my way to the airport bathroom. I needed to get dressed in a full gown and do my hair and makeup in ten minutes. I sat on top of the counter and slapped on some rouge and lipstick and teased my hair high, which was appropriate in 1993. I could tell that the women walking into the bathroom were wondering why a hooker was getting dressed in the airport bathroom. I didn't care. With sweat dripping down my face, I pulled a red dress out of my purse and put it on. It was the only thing I had brought with me because as soon as I was done with the signing I was headed back to L.A. I dragged my limp body to the car and collapsed in the backseat as the driver drove me to the convention center.

Once I got there they put me in a chair with a stack of pictures and a marker. I knew I just had to make it through this and then I could go home. I prayed to God at that moment that He would make men not interested in a blonde with big boobs wearing a tight red gown, but divine intervention was not on my side that day. As soon as they opened the line, groups of men stormed in with their cameras and sweaty grins. I dove in and started taking pictures and signing autographs, sometimes on their body parts. It was getting really crowded and cameras were flashing all around me. Things started to get blurry as sweat began pouring down my face. I continued to push on and tried really hard to shake off whatever was happening to my body, but I couldn't. My body started to tremble all over, and people finally stopped taking pictures because they could now see that SOMETHING WAS WRONG with this bimbo in a dress. I tried to mumble "Help" but couldn't. I slowly stood up with at least two hundred men staring at me and . . . then it happened. The demon within me came out and I CRAPPED all over my dress! Liquid poo shot out of my butt and all over the back of my dress. The looks on these men's faces were unlike anything I had ever seen. I guess I was predicting my future at this point of being able to turn men on and gross them out just as much. I screamed, "OH MY GOD!!"

as loud as I could and ran to the bathroom. I could not bear to look behind me and witness the trail I had left behind. Men to this day have come up to me to tell me that they heard about or were even there on this dreadful day. Needless to say, this has been burned into my memory and will continue to haunt me at every future autograph session for the rest of my life.

If you've read my other books you know that I seemed to be plagued by poo. Some might think I'm obsessed with talking about it and that could be true. I think because I have had so many problems with it, I have to find the humor in it. Let's face it. Sometimes poop is funny. On that note, here's my second most embarrassing story. Enjoy.

The second boyfriend I ever had I nicknamed "Chunkman." Named after his chunky belly, even though he always thought it was his chunky penis. Shh. Don't tell him. The moment I met him I thought I was going to marry him. He was very Zen and had beautiful philosophies on life, probably because of the enormous amount of pot he smoked. Anyway, he lit candles all over the room and put some Pink Floyd on the stereo. This was going to be our first romantic rendezvous. He kissed me passionately and played with my breasts for a whole fifteen minutes! Who does that anymore? Anyway, I couldn't wait for him to rip off my pants and go down on me. He slowly made his way there, teasing every inch before the panties came off. Once they did he smiled lovingly at me and then dove in. He was doing quite well for a boy in college until he started coughing while down there. He looked like he was a little embarrassed by the coughing, so I showed him how it wasn't bothering me by spreading my legs even further. He then shot up from between my legs, gasping for air. I said, "What's the matter?"

He replied, "You have a dingleberry hanging off your butt. I'm sorry, but I was trying to hold my breath."

I ran into the bathroom, and sure enough, he was right. I wanted God to take me away and save me from this horrid nightmare, but he didn't. Instead I started crying and told "Chunkman" to go home. We did see each other after that, but you can be damn sure my ass was so clean you could have eaten dinner off it.

So if you ever get caught in one of life's embarrassing moments, reflect on mine, because I'm sure it will make you feel better. Life always has a way of keeping you in check, even if you THINK you look hot in a red dress or smell like roses.

Going at It Alone

I know some women who have gone through divorce feel as if they have failed. I think the reason I stayed in my own marriage longer than I should have was because I never quit at anything I start. I always give my all to everything I do. How could I bow out of something so sacred, especially when there was a child involved? I can't believe today that I still had the guts to go through with it, but in the end I never felt as good about myself as I do today.

The last time I was single was when I was twelve years old. I was one of those girls who had the next boyfriend lined up before I broke up with the one I was with. Being alone was something I was deathly afraid of. Wait, let me correct that. Being alone is still something I'm afraid of. I always morphed myself into the person I thought I should be for the man I was dating. This left me with little sense of self. So I never really got to just sit and face my own shit.

Your partner in life should complement who you are, *not* reflect who you are. I was such a caretaker that I would constantly try to help the other person because it seemed so much easier than fixing myself. I thought if he would just be happy, then I would be happy. Boy, is that bullshit. There's that whole spiritual philosophy that people who insult and put down other people are actually saying it to themselves. I believe this to be true. They are miserable inside, so they point the finger at everyone else, hoping it will make them feel more secure. In my case, I would do the opposite. I would try so hard to pick people up, hoping it would do the same for me. It never really did.

I've been on my own for a few months now, and I'm slowly getting used to "going at it alone." There are times in bed when I miss having a hairy foot to rub against or someone to yell at when I feel crabby, but all in all, it's nice to just worry about my own feelings. I still don't understand the concept of "figuring out who you are," but I'm sure in time I will have watched enough episodes of *Oprah* to grasp it.

For those women out there who are divorced and are still carrying around the slightest feeling of failure, please, for the love of God, throw it down the garbage disposal. Get rid of it! Fry it up in a pan and feed it the dogs. I'm looking at this new journey as a victory. It's time to start over and feel empowered about who I am. If you feel like a failure, you will become one. If you feel like a winner, the world will open up so many opportunities you won't know which door to choose. Damn, I sound like a fortune cookie.

Good luck out there to the ladies who need a pick-me-up. Remember, you're not alone. Jennifer Aniston, Uma Thurman, and Jessica Simpson are also in the divorcée club. So hold your head up high and don't worry about trying to find that hairy foot to lie next to at night. You need to worry about yourself, and the right hairy foot will come along when it's supposed to.

The Power of the Pussy

Everyone has a different name for it. I like to call it poontango and sometimes canooter. I think when you name it something cute, it makes it sound prettier. It makes you think it might have curtains on it with some welcoming throw pillows, like the inside of Jeannie's bottle. Whatever you do call it, it is truly the one and only thing that rules mankind. If it wasn't for the power of the pussy, women would still not be allowed to vote and some man never would have invented the dishwasher. Think about it, if we don't get shit done, we are not happy. If we are not happy, we don't put out. So throughout history there was always some wife using her pussy as collateral to get shit done. Not LITERALLY, of course. I don't think Rosa Parks flashed her canooter to get a seat at the front of the bus. But we all know the one thing most men want, and thank God we are holding the key.

Let's talk about the actual vagina for a second. I never really figured out the plumbing until I was much older. I was scared to even look at it. It seemed wrong to actually take a mirror and check it out, and when I finally did in my teens I was horrified. I didn't understand why men found it so sexy. It just looked like a couple of pieces of bologna. And then there are some women who have outies and others have innies. An innie is when the clitoris is kind of hidden away under a hood, and the outie is when the hood door is left open. After watching Pamela Anderson's porno I couldn't help but notice she has an innie. I hated the fact that not only does she have a perfect body but even her pussy could have its own monthly calendar. I have an outie and have always been kind of embarrassed by it 'cause it just seems like a messy deli counter. A bunch of meat shoved around on display.

Anyway, it amazes me that some men are really good at maneuvering their way around there and some are so bad you're actually embarrassed for them. In the past I've noticed that explaining it to them during their voyage down under can really help. Shouting things like "RIGHT THERE!" (because they licked off half your thigh just trying to find the spot) and "KEEP DOING IT JUST LIKE THAT!" (because if you don't tell them to keep up with that motion they will do eighty different types of magic tricks with fingers and tongues that won't let you get to the finish line). Consistency in motion is key in this department. Also, if you feel your guy kind of gets it and kind of doesn't, try talking to him about it. It's much better than having to lie upside down with your legs around your neck just so he can find the spot.

Now let's talk about grooming your canooter. It's very common to have the hair down below at least mowed or waxed monthly. The most common method is shaving and then just trimming the foyer carpet. About five years ago, the trend was just to leave a small, straight patch. Nowadays, it's barren as a desert. Girls are shaving it all off. If you are reading this and have never done a trim down there, for God's sake, girlfriend, go get some scissors and start cutting. It's hard enough for guys to maneuver there, and if you leave a jungle to try and get through I would get lost, too. We're not in the caveman days anymore, when women needed to have pubic hair to keep dirt out as they sat on the earth without any fig leaves.

We've got underwear now and douches, so shave it off! It's also a good thing to do if you ever want to surprise your husband. It could actually be the best and cheapest birthday gift you could give him if you've never been barren before. I used to have a smooth runway, but now I am forced to grow out a foyer carpet to cover my C-section scar. But I still keep the landing strip smooth.

So the next time your man thinks he holds the power, simply spread your legs and watch him fall to his knees. The power of the pussy will never be overthrown!

Life's Pet Peeves

W here in the hell did this name come from? We all know what it refers to, but why anyone said, "That asshole is chewing with his mouth open and it really annoys me. Hey, I've got the perfect name for it. I'm going to call it a pet peeve!" I'm sure if I did some homework on it and looked it up I would find the origin, but this is not that kind of book. I just want to bitch about them, not see if the expression "pet peeves" might be buried in the Bible code somewhere.

I checked out most of my pet peeves with my friends just to make sure they resembled some of theirs. The conversation sounded like my friends were having orgasms. Whenever I would say something, all you heard on the other end of the phone was "OH, YES, YES, YES!"

I found that most of my pet peeves were in the supermarket. As a mother or wife you find yourself inside the damn market almost every day. Just being there is a pet peeve and then add old people to it and it really is hell on earth. Let's go right to the deli counter. I pull a number and see that I'm number eighty, but the sign says they are only on number sixty-five. Unfortunately, number sixty-five is a granny who is asking to taste-test the pastrami. There are fifteen people behind Granny with laser beams shooting from their eyes into Grandma's head. I'm sure you can all guess what Granny does next. That's right, she asks to taste the cheese. Now if you're that old, I'm sure you've tasted Swiss cheese somewhere in your eighty years of life. Swiss cheese tastes like Swiss cheese. Move on, Grandma. There's four generations of people behind you!!!

Let's move on to the aisles now. I hate hate hate when a person has his or her cart in the middle of the aisle blocking your way to move forward. I have politely said, "Excuse me," and it drives me insane when they do

NOTHING! They are so caught up in reading the labels of their favorite canned foods that they have no idea they've caused a traffic jam.

Now it's time to get rung up. I don't know about your grocery store, but there are twelve checkout stands at mine, and every time I go there, they have only TWO open. There's always about fifteen people in each line and of course someone always pulls out a checkbook to pay for their food when your screaming baby has been in line for twenty minutes. This is the world of ATMs now, people. Unless you're married to Fred Flintstone, you should try and get with the times.

Another biggie of mine is when someone is talking to me and someone else walks up and asks me a question while I am listening to one conversation already. My head bops back and forth, not knowing who to answer first. UGH!

I also hate when people are intensely making out in public places. Teenagers are okay, but if you have boobs that have moved passed the belly button region and your husband resembles Santa, please don't slip him the tongue in public places.

Last but not least is when I'm trying to make a left turn and the car in front of me won't move up into the middle of the intersection. They hang back, waiting for the light to turn yellow, only allowing THEIR OWN CAR TO TURN LEFT. I HATE IT!!

Okay, I'm done screaming, but if you are in front of me in any deli counter line I highly suggest NOT asking to taste the cheese or I might just have to cut the cheese on you!

His New Girlfriend

For those of you who are still successfully married, you won't really be able to relate to this chapter, but you are more than welcome to live vicariously through my own pain in this situation. I have yet to include a new man in my life, but John has already gotten himself a girlfriend. It's still relatively new, so I'm not interested in meeting her yet. I'm sure there will be quite a few of these "sperm banks" before he settles on a bank he wants to be inside for more than a week. So needless to say, I'm in no hurry to make an introduction to the first one.

The first awkward thing that happened was that he came to me and asked me for some girlfriend advice. I mean, come ON! I looked at him like he was on crack. Then a few weeks later, he felt like he needed to share intimate sexual details with me. I plugged my ears and started shouting "LALALALALALA!" The weird thing is that I'm not jealous in the least bit, but hearing him talk about sex with someone else is like a brother telling you how he went down on a chick. When I asked him why he felt the need to share this "vagina sandwich" story with me, he said that I was his best friend and he thought it wouldn't bother me. I told him to find a best friend with a penis who would enjoy hearing about a girl who can make her vagina sing songs. Personally, I think he's testing me to see if I get jealous, but it's not working. I really do hope he finds someone he cares about someday, but for Pete's sake, I've got my own vagina. I don't want to hear about anybody else's.

This past weekend I wanted to go to this designer warehouse sale, so I called John up at the last minute to see if he would babysit. He barked for a minute and then agreed only if I would buy his "sperm bank" a pair of jeans. I quickly said yes, told him to hurry up, and then hung up the phone. It took me a second to realize what he had just asked me to do. He had asked me to buy something for HIS girlfriend. OH, MY GOD. When he got to my house I told him I wasn't sure if they made jeans for loose vaginas but I would look. He snickered and then blurted out that she was a size 24. A size 24? Who in the hell is a size 24? I've never in my life known anyone who fit into a size 24. I said, "What is she, sixteen?" He blurted, "No, she's just skinny."

"Or a coke whore." I giggled and walked out the door.

Once I took care of my own shopping discount spree I wandered over to the bulimic jean sizes. As I searched the rack I was surprised to see that they even made women's jeans in this size. I held a pair up to myself and noticed that the thigh portion of the jean covered only half my thigh. I thought maybe this girl might not have been born with a quad muscle. It was really the only other explanation besides the bulimic, coke whore, or being sixteen scenario. As I continued to look, I found myself struggling yet again with which kind of jeans to get her. Do I buy her an ugly pair so she looks like shit in them? But if I do, then she'll think I have really bad taste, and if I buy her a really cool pair she'll think my taste is awesome but unfortunately look incredibly hot. Now that you guys have gotten to know me, which jeans do you think I went with? That's right, I went with the ugly ones. I came back home and handed them to John, and he examined them.

He said, "Are rhinestones on jeans 'in' right now?"

I replied, "Totally, especially these ones, because the rhinestones are shaped into butterflies."

"Cool," he said.

With that, he left, and I smiled, knowing that not even Kate Moss could make those jeans look good.

So I'm sure I'm headed into more situations that involve new "sperm banks" as time goes on. I'll just deal with them as they come, but if he ever asks me to buy something for his girlfriend again I'll reply, "Sure, but maybe on your way over you wouldn't mind picking up a large cock ring for my new boyfriend." Okay, maybe I am a little jealous.

Death Becomes You

I can't do a book about life and not mention death. It's an inevitable event that will happen to all of us—we just hope much later rather than sooner. My dream death scenario would be when I'm about eighty-seven years old and I lie down to take a nap and never wake up. How awesome would that be?

I still have a hard time with the concept of open-casket ceremonies. I can't imagine someone painting makeup on my face after my eyelids and mouth have been glued shut. I will be so pissed off if my loved ones do not nail my coffin shut and just put adorable pictures of me up and tell humorous stories about me. I would much rather have people listen to a story about how I crapped myself at an autograph signing than to compliment how the formaldehyde is really keeping things together.

Now that I am a mother, dying takes on a whole new meaning. I'm not scared about death whatsoever because of my beliefs in the afterlife. I just have to take better responsibility for my own health so I can be with my boy as long as I physically can. When I was in college, I was a real risk taker. I skydived, slept with weirdos, drank till I puked, and popped stuff into my mouth that would "open doors" to new dimensions. Now I'm afraid to take aspirin. I can't imagine doing anything that would jeopardize my future with my son, which was the number-one reason I quit smoking.

If you haven't made out your will, you'd better get your ass on it. Some people are spooked out by doing it, but it's better to be safe than sorry. I was amazed to find out that, at least in California, if you leave your money to your spouse, he or she does not have to pay taxes on it, but when you leave it to your children, they do have to pay taxes on it. That's such bullshit. It's crazy to me that you would get taxed again on anything that you have AL-

READY paid taxes on. Ugh! Oprah needs to run for president. The country would be a much better place.

Escaping death is something I can say I've already done many times. If cats really do have nine lives, then I should be spitting up fur balls and crapping in a litterbox in my house. My biggest near-death experience happened to me on my very first episode of MTV's *Singled Out.* We shot our first show during spring break, and I was forced to stay in a crappy puke-filled hotel the night before. Speaking of puke, my boyfriend at the time was with me and was suffering from the stomach flu. I had to get some serious sleep because this was going to be my television debut, and I thought it would be nice if I left a candle burning for him in the bathroom. This way he could see where his puke was going while being romantically lit. I, of course, was snoring logs in bed getting my beauty sleep.

The next thing I know I'm dreaming of this angel floating toward me, screaming, "Jenny, wake up!" I kept telling her this was the best sleep of my life and she kept screaming, "JENNY, WAKE UP!" I honestly was so incredibly comfortable I kept arguing with this woman floating around my face. "Please leave me alone. I'm sleeping so peacefully." The screams became so angry that I had no other choice but to open one of my eyes. As soon as I did, I became confused by what I saw. I lay there paralyzed by the intensity of black smoke that surrounded me and saw in horror that the ceiling above my head was engulfed in flames. I was amazed that the fire made no sound yet the entire ceiling above me looked like the gates of hell. I started screaming to my boyfriend to wake up, and I was hitting him because I knew he was getting into that death sleep that I had been entering into. After I hit him a few times he opened his eyes and in one breath dragged me out of the room into the hallway. As soon as we plopped down, firemen were showing up and climbed over us to get to the flames. Our entire bodies were black. We were coughing up chunks of black smoke and were told five more minutes and we would have died in our sleep. Now I understand why people don't die because of the flames in a fire. The smoke takes you to a very peaceful place that you really do not want to wake up from.

If you can believe it, I still had to shoot my first episode of *Singled Out* that day. I did it with as much life as I could muster, all the while continuing to cough up black chunks. I visited the room the next day and still couldn't believe I had survived. There were no walls left and everything was black. I learned a few valuable lessons from all of this. One is, always check and make sure the smoke detectors work in any hotel room you are staying in, and number two, don't leave a candle burning, thinking that your sick boyfriend is going to blow it out after he is done puking for the night.

So even though at times you might think you are inde- structible, death is inevitable. If you take good care of yourself and live the best life you can, maybe you can stretch it out a few extra years. And if you're really lucky, you've got a bigmouthed guardian angel watching out for you along the way.

Singled Out

I t's so bizarre to me that I'm open for business again in the dating world. My biggest rise to fame was on a dating game show called *Singled Out*. I was the confident, ball-busting, in-your-face chick who seemed secure enough to scare the shit out of the cockiest of men. But truthfully, when it comes to first dates, I am as nervous as the rest of them. It's scarier now that I have a three-year-old son and want to protect him from anyone I date until

I truly believe the man is worthy. I feel like now that I am older, not only do I have "baggage" with me but C-section scars and stretch marks that only a husband could love. I have no idea what another guy will think of my birthing wounds since he was not there to witness me trying to deliver my son into this world. I'm sure I'm completely stretched out down there also, and I'm afraid that the guy will feel like he is having sex with a hallway.

Along with those pretty attributes, I'm afraid of learning somebody's likes and dislikes all over again. I'm also scared of game playing and, scariest of all, I'm afraid of falling in love and getting hurt. I rushed it the last time, and I don't want it to happen again. On the selfish side, what happens if I fall in love with a guy who has a chopstick for a penis? What if he thinks my deflated boobs look like zucchinis? What if he sees my ring-around-the-ass and is totally turned off? I guess all you can do is trust who you are and hope that someone sees past the boo-boos on your body along with the ones in your heart, but that's a lot easier said than done.

It's been a few months since my divorce, and I went out on my first date just recently. I wish you could have seen how nervous I was. I called every person I know to get advice. I got waxed, a manicure, and even headed to the salon for a blow-dry. On my way to his house I had butterflies in my belly. I listened to Barry Manilow on the radio and bit my newly manicured nails off daydreaming about what lies ahead for me in this game of life. I wasn't driving there dreaming he was "the one," I was just hoping for a little company and some food for the soul. Okay, maybe a little French kissing, but nothing else.

I pulled into his driveway and looked in the mirror to check my lip-gloss status. I couldn't help but notice the smile on my face. It had been a long time since I had looked that happy. It's amazing that happiness made me look younger than BOTOX. I was definitely on the right path. I opened my car door and walked up his stairs. I stared at his door for at least five minutes before I rang the bell. The butterflies were out of control again, and I felt my armpits draining out like two hoses. I closed my eyes and told myself to relax and be myself. I deserved some happiness and hopefully this was going to be the start of it. I opened my eyes with a smile and reached for the bell. Before my finger even hit the button the door whisked open . . .

To be continued . . .

Life's Little Sayings

Here are a few of my favorite quotes.

Take into account that great love and great achievements involve great risk.

—Dalai Lama

How old would you be if you didn't know how old you are?

—Satchel Paige

Remember that the best relationship is one in which your love for each other exceeds your need for each other.

—Dalai Lama

Don't wait for your "ship to come in," and feel angry and cheated when it doesn't. Get going with something small.

—Irene Kassorla

When you lose, don't lose the lesson.

—Dalai Lama

A man would prefer to come home to an unmade bed and a happy woman than to a neatly made bed and an angry woman.

—Marlene Dietrich

Don't knock masturbation—it's sex with someone I love.

—Woody Allen

Women:

Women are like apples on trees. The best ones are at the top of the tree. Most men don't want to reach for the good ones because they are afraid of falling and getting hurt.

Instead, they sometimes take apples from the ground that aren't as good, but easy. The apples at the top think something is wrong with them, when in reality, they're amazing. They just have to wait for the right man to come along, the one who's brave enough to climb all the way to the top of the tree.

Men:

Men are like fine wine. They begin as grapes, and it's up to women to stomp the shit out of them until they turn into something acceptable to have dinner with.

—Unknown

About the Author

Jenny McCarthy is the *New York Times* bestselling author of *Baby Laughs: The Naked Truth About the First Year of Mommyhood* and *Belly Laughs: The Naked Truth About Pregnancy and Childbirth*. She lives in California with her son, Evan.

The author will donate a portion of her proceeds from this book to Talk About Curing Autism (TACA), a nonprofit organization that is focused on building the autism community by connecting people, families, friends, and professionals and sharing information that can help children with autism be the best they can be. To donate or learn more, visit TACAnow.com.